CW01669386

CONTENTS

21 CHAPTERS FOR THE 21ST CENTURY'S CHANGING WORLD

Edition 2

Publication Date: 20th August, 2020

A Part of REGENT GROUP

INTRODUCTION

Dr Selva Pankaj is the CEO and co-founder of Regent Group – a global education, real estate and investment management organisation headquartered in London.

Selva qualified as a chartered management accountant in the early 1990s before completing an MBA. He then attended both London Business School and Harvard Business School for an Executive Education programme. In 2019 he was awarded an Honorary Doctorate from the University of Bolton. The Higher Doctorate, Doctor of Education (Hon EdD) award is the highest academic distinction available within any UK university. In addition, he received a Post Honorary Doctorate from Azteca University, Mexico in June 2019.

It was while studying at Harvard that eminent scholar Professor Clayton M. Christensen, told him: "You have got to know who you are and learn to differentiate between man-made laws and the laws of nature."

At first, Selva did not understand this; but it aroused his curiosity and led him to seek out and study great literature from authors including Dr Napoleon Hill, Earl Nightingale, Wallace D Wattles and Thomas Troward, in relation to human potential, human behaviour and success. Those teachings, and the work of Bob Proctor – also a world-renowned speaker, educational coach and author, changed Selva's life dramatically, as did working within Bob's Inner Circle.

Together with his wife Tharshiny and his late father Senior Selvanayagam, Selva Pankaj founded Regent Group in 2000. The business started with one private tuition student generating £20/ hour and has since grown into a multi-million-pound company, with a diverse portfolio of educational, real estate and investment management divisions.

During that time, the three founders conceived the Regent Group ethos, "The end of education is character" - the valued principle behind Selva Pankaj's inspiration for writing this book. The philosophy was introduced in 2000 and now, nearly 20 years later, has been proven and validated with the "Thinking into Character" transformational leadership/change management programme and this book.

Regent Group specialises in education and Selva and Tharshiny are incredibly proud to have educated tens of thousands of students, helping them to achieve their potential and attain great educational and career success. It now operates in the UK, Canada, United States, India and Dubai with a global focus and the goal of creating a British university with UK degree-awarding powers; its educational pedagogy is underpinned by the philosophies of Dr Napoleon Hill and the

Carnegie Foundation, using educational science to accelerate learning and global peace and unity.

We believe that this university will not only enable affordable education within the UK, but also act as a beacon of positive mental attitude and aspiration, offering British degrees all over the world. Global communities may not initially dream about this magnificent gift; however, with such British generosity and encouragement, the world will become a better place for future generations, offering peace, harmony, prosperity, unity and success. This global reach is now a reality as the fourth educational revolution and artificial intelligence change the higher education landscape in the 21st century. This book has 21 chapters to enable change in the 21st century: our changing world.

The 21 chapters are in harmony with the natural laws of growth, they provide an incremental, sequential, highly integrated approach to the creation of success and interpersonal effectiveness. Using them can help us to move progressively from dependence to independence to inter-dependence.

Selva and Tharshiny have also set up the Regent Education Trust, a charity to promote education in developing countries that is committed to giving every child the opportunity to be educated, grow in confidence and achieve their full potential. It is involved in several educational, social welfare and charitable projects across South Asia and Africa. They also host an Annual Global Unity Forum to promote forgiveness and unity among different communities. For peace and forgiveness, they also promote an initiative called Harmony House, as an interfaith forum.

FOREWORD

BY BOB PROCTOR, BEST-SELLING AUTHOR OF *YOU WERE BORN RICH* AND FEATURED TEACHER IN THE SECRET

Johann Wolfgang von Goethe said: "Before you can do something you must first be something." I love that quote, and I've shared it hundreds of times with people all over the world.

So, when I found out that Dr. Selva Pankaj had written a book called Thinking into Character, I was excited to write the foreword because he has more character than most of the people I know. In other words, Selva didn't just write a book about character; he demonstrates it in his personal and professional life every day.

Character is so important to Selva, demonstrated by the fact that his global educational organization is founded on the principle that The end of education is character. So, if you're interested in developing character, you're reading the right book.

There are many gems to reap from Thinking Into Character, but the one thing that really sticks out for me is the way Selva ties character to your dreams and setting goals that are right for you.

After helping you set a goal that is unique and worthy of you, Selva leads you through a proven process for creating success by working towards something that you love.

As you read this book, you'll get an inside-out education; enhancing your character by controlling your mind - keeping it busy with a definite purpose, a worthy goal and an organised plan, which Napoleon Hill wrote about in Think & Grow Rich.

Carry this book in your back pocket. Let it become your faithful friend that nudges you, at every point in your journey, to unlock your potential.

No matter where you are in life—working towards an educational goal, launching a product, service, or business, longing for a better relationship, or building wealth—developing your character by focusing on a worthy ideal adds a whole new dimension to life. It makes you feel alive and excited to get out of bed each morning.

Thinking into Character raises your level of conscious awareness. And as your level of awareness rises, you'll realize you are capable of achieving anything you want.

Your adventure lies ahead and Thinking into Character is a must-have resource for building your best life!

"The mind is the master power that moulds and makes; and [man/women] is mind and evermore [he/she] takes the tool of thought and shaping what [he/she] wills, brings forth a thousand joys, a thousand ills. [He/she] thinks in secret and it comes to pass, environment is but his looking glass."

"They themselves are makers of themselves. By virtue of the thoughts which humans choose and encourage; that mind is the master weaver, both of the inner garment of character, and the outer garment of circumstance, and that as they may have hitherto woven in ignorance and pain they may now weave in enlightenment and happiness."

James Allen, As a Man Thinketh

PRAISE FOR

THINKING INTO CHARACTER

"Life shows you the path in multiple ways. I had the great fortune to have Selva illuminating mine a few years ago. What a great life example of the power of the human being to lead himself into greatness despite obstacles; from very challenging beginnings to the summit of a professional and personal career. The integration of business seasoned background, deep humanistic approach, solid intellectual and academic foundations and a willingness to make an impact, make Selva a unique mirror in which to reflect. I could not be happier than having the world enjoy his elixir of character in his book and sharing in unique experiences through the lenses of a giant like Selva."

Carlos Escario

Partner, Huete & Co

"I have enjoyed every word of Selva's manuscript ***Thinking into Character*** beginning with the foreword by Bob Procter who featured in The Secret based on the book which has affected the lives of so many millions in this world. This book is a must for anyone looking for positivity which is the key for success. It is a great tool to strengthen the power of mind and have a positive mental attitude by teaching the formula for success through a positive mental attitude. One particular sentence caught my attention: The mind controls the body and the body is an instrument of the mind. I have known Selva for some time, he is one of the most charismatic individuals I have ever met. His book will become the companion of every person aiming for success."

Prof Nadey Hakim GCStJ, MD, PhD, Hon D.Arts
President's Envoy, Imperial College London, Chevalier de la Legion d'Honneur

"***Thinking into Character*** sizzles with authenticity and innovation. Armed with a voracious passion for standing at the forefront of the global education model, Selva takes you on a compelling ride where you discover an inside out perspective into the powers of your own mind. I loved the inspiring and thought provoking candour of this book. An indispensable blueprint that will show you how to build the tools that will help you reach your lifelong dreams."

Lyle Sopel
President of Sopel Studio Inc / Global Arts Vision

"Professional success without personal fulfilment is the ultimate failure. This book masterfully brings us to the roots of fulfilment: character based on truth and values. Values + a will to bring them to life = virtues. If we want to have a better society and better institutions we need more leaders thinking and building their character. This book will definitely help."

Luis Huete
Founder, Huete & Co

"It is normally a difficult task to write an endorsement for any book. However, in the case of ***Thinking into Character***, it was a very easy task because the writer is someone who, like me, started life from very humble beginnings and knows what it takes to achieve success. This book is a chronicle of personal experiences going back many decades.

I am delighted to add my name to the series, and I consider it a 'must read' for those who aspire to rise in their lives. ***Thinking into Character*** provides a structured and practical approach to the key principles to help us become even more successful in our chosen fields. In fact, we often overlook structuring our approach to maximise results out of the opportunities that life presents us. We sometimes also fail to identify and as a result, do not achieve our goals.

Thinking into Character highlights such points, helping us to achieve what is important for us. I particularly admire the step-by-step approach adopted in this series, which provides clarity of Selva's thinking and logic. I am sure that readers will find the contents immensely inspiring, interesting and useful. The contents of the book reminded me of my own humble journey when I began my business from a shed with just £2 capital. The steps I took over the years, which were taken on key principles highlighted within these books, made my company, Sun Mark Ltd, the most decorated company in Britain through winning an unprecedented five consecutive Queens Awards for Enterprise in International Trade.

I admire Selva; he is a passionate and highly talented individual who cares for everybody and likes to put back into society from where we benefit. I am sure you will enjoy learning from these books as much as I have."

Dr Rami Ranger CBE
Chairman, Sun Mark Ltd

"Every time I meet Selva he both impresses and surprises me. He is an original thinker who doesn't walk away from a challenge. He arrived in this country with very little of material worth, but he had a unique and bright mind coupled with relentless tenacity. Here he has been generous enough to share with us his philosophy and the experiences that contributed to his success."

Dr Maurizio Bragagni MBA
CEO, Tratos

"***Thinking into Character*** teaches you how to identify and truly focus upon your goal. It leaves no question as to the necessity of emotional involvement in the journey. This resonated with me on a personal basis as I knew that I had to be precise about where I wanted to get to when building my career. I hope that others will heed Selva's wise words; it will pay dividends."

Simon Blagden CBE
Non-executive Chairman, Fujitsu UK

"At a time when we are increasingly ill-preparing today's youth for the employment challenges of tomorrow – including, for example, those challenges presented by Artificial Intelligence as highlighted by the All-Party Parliamentary Group on the Fourth Industrial Revolution – it is refreshing to read this text which powerfully champions the importance of positivity in achieving success.

There will always be detractors of self-help books, but the roots of this book stem from the widely acclaimed works of Sir Anthony Seldon, the University of Buckingham's Vice-Chancellor, who is one of the greatest educators of our generation. Sir Anthony's original thinking figures heavily in Selva's work, as do other world-renowned educators and innovators, to enhance modern-day thinking as we struggle for understanding and achievement.

The difference between success and failure is small. Indeed, there are those who passionately proclaim that you cannot achieve success without having experienced failure. This book helps readers to learn about themselves and progress through a methodology of approach that heightens knowledge, shares experiences and promises to improve effectiveness.

Some of the case studies and anecdotes included by Selva really resonate and I would challenge anyone not to take some benefit from his insightful approach. If you are impatient, however, I might encourage you to follow me and begin at the end, reading the chapters in reverse order. Starting as you mean to achieve your goals and working backwards to fill in the missing gaps makes for great character, demonstrating that we are all different and there are many ways to stand out from a crowd."

Ronel Lehmann

Founder and Chief Executive, Finito Education Ltd

"I operate a large chain of McDonald's restaurants across north and west London as well as in Berkshire and Buckinghamshire, serving more than 28 million customers each year. As a businessman employing more than 3,000 people, I have grown to appreciate more and more the increasing pressures that we can all face in our lives.

Thinking into Character teaches you how to combat these challenges. Selva's book is nothing short of revolutionary: transforming the way you think, encouraging you to focus on what goals matter to you and helping you to discover for yourself how to reach them.

We all have skills and talents which are yet to be unlocked, hurdles we are yet to jump, as well as things we don't know about ourselves. ***Thinking into Character*** – by teaching you to do away with negative self-images, to open your mind and to think freely – transforms the way you see yourself and pushes you to new limits. I whole-heartedly recommend this marvellous piece of writing to anybody who wants to achieve in life."

Atul Pathak OBE
MD of APPT Corporation

"Selva, my husband and business partner, is passionate about ***Thinking into Character***. He lives and breathes it. He has personally experienced the benefits of the TiC philosophy and I have been there and witnessed first-hand the positive way in which it has changed him. He is more focused, more driven and yet at the same time, less stressed about achieving his goals.

I have no doubt that by following the same programme, the lives of others can be positively changed in this manner!"

Tharshiny Pankaj
Managing Director, Regent Group

"***Thinking into Character*** is innovative, ground-breaking and comprehensive – it covers a wide range of topics in depth with unique perspectives on key areas. Many of the issues covered are those which often "get in the way of learning", such as a lack of proper goal setting or understanding of the importance of ambition to success itself. It covers mental health and individual beliefs, and helps to address feelings of unworthiness. Often these difficult to tackle issues are the cause of problems regarding retention and progression and can affect an individual's prospects of success. There is a huge amount of incredibly valuable content, and this is broken down into a digestible set of chapters to take on board. The content is inclusive and will be easy to adopt by a variety of readers."

Professor G E Holmes DL
President & Vice Chancellor, The University of Bolton,
Greater Manchester

A MESSAGE FROM THE AUTHOR

Dear Reader,

I would first like to thank you for making a committed decision to read this book. I am honoured that the thoughts I have written here, may lead you to make significant changes in your way of thinking, and in turn bring greater success and contentment to your life.

The messages contained within have taught me so much; I believe I am a better, wiser person for it. I believe they will do the same for you. I read this book every day and I am learning every day as well.

I believe self-discovery and the betterment of one's self, to be an on-going challenge. To that end, I would truly be delighted to hear from you with your views on this book - your experiences and successes based on the lessons contained within.

I whole heartedly believe this book should not be categorised as a one-off read and left on a shelf to gather dust or banished to the bottom of your e-book folder. The information is designed to be a companion for life-long learning in the continuous process of a change in habits and achievement of growth and indeed success. This is also supplemented by the access to the Thinking into Character Virtual Campus for video/audio lessons and worksheets. Success is a progressive realisation of a worthy goal. Success means very different things to each of us and we need to think about success in relation to achieving self-fulfilment.

As you progress into a deeper level of understanding and implementation, you can go back time and time again to principles contained in each chapter, and the video/audio lessons on the Thinking into Character platform.

Once you understand these principles, take an inside-out approach. Study with the purpose of sharing or discussing what you learn with someone else as soon as you are ready to help others. You will be ready by the time you finish reading the book.

I guarantee that if you approach the material and lessons in each chapter and on the virtual platform in this way, you will not only remember what you study, but your perspective and awareness will be expanded; your understanding deepened, and your motivation to implement the 'learning' will exponentially increase. You need to spontaneously give and graciously receive the rewards.

Your growth will at first be evolutionary but the net effect over time will be revolutionary. If you decide to open your mind to really understand and live the principles embodied in the

Thinking into Character book and programme, I would feel humbly comfortable in assuming that many positive things will happen for you.

Character is a composite of habits; 'sow a thought, reap an action, so an action, reap a habit, sow a habit, reap a character, sow a character, reap a destiny which is the creation of success and self-fulfilment.

I am contactable via selva@rtc.uk.net

I wish you the very best on your personal journey, and do keep 'thinking'.

Dr Selva Pankaj

"To our daughters, Sharanie and Dharanie…

Whilst writing this book, I have often thought of you both. Life is, and always will be, full of challenges. The natural laws and practices in this book, whilst meaning little to you now, will, I trust, guide you as you grow into young women and make your place in the world.

Putting Thinking into Character together has been a heartening experience and I know that in time, this book will come to mean as much to you as it does to me."

CHAPTER 1

A WORTHY GOAL

Welcome to *Thinking into Character*. This book is based on several sources derived from my studies at London Business School and Harvard Business School, under the leadership of Prof Clayton M. Christensen, and on the teachings of Bob Proctor, Earl Nightingale, Napoleon Hill, Wallace D. Wattles, Thomas Troward and many other authors.

These learnings are further under-pinned by teachings from the late Stephen Hawking, Richard Branson, Elon Musk, Andrew Carnegie, Albert Einstein, Henry Ford, Isaac Newton and Steve Jobs, the late Apple co-founder. The list goes on.

This book further explores the educational philosophy conceived by Andrew Carnegie, who asked Napoleon Hill to dedicate his life to studying successful people in the world in the 1930s.

These concepts have resulted in millions of people becoming very successful and achieving self-fulfilment.

Napoleon Hill's teaching was then adapted by Earl Nightingale and I have adapted much of Nightingale's wisdom into this book, alongside legend Bob Proctor, who has taken me, and countless others, to a different level of understanding and awareness.

Napoleon Hill's son, Blair, was a great source of inspiration to him in terms of success and character. Although Blair was born without ears, and his doctor said that he would never be able to hear or speak, Blair grew up able to hear and speak almost normally.

Hill is quoted as saying: "If a person has built a sound character, it makes but little difference what people say about [him/her], because [he/she] will win in the end."

What is character? The *Oxford Dictionary* defines character as: "The mental and moral qualities distinctive to an individual." Mental activity is linked to our mind. In the context of this book, we are looking at building your character through the repetition of thoughts, feelings and actions. Someone with a good character lives their life and makes their decisions in a manner that is honest, respectful and responsible.

Making mistakes does not mean you do not have good character. But, when someone of good character makes a mistake, they take ownership of it. They hold honourable principles, which means they make good choices and do the right thing, even when it is difficult.

Good character is the key to persevering with your goals when others give up at the first or second hurdle. The outcome of a good character is the positive results you achieve in your personal life, your education and your professional and personal career.

When I talk about character, understand this: it is what we think and our feelings, thoughts and actions that ultimately manifest themselves as character and in turn create our results.

One of the most valuable concepts that this philosophy has taught me is the importance of setting goals. Not just any goal. Not a goal you know how to achieve. I'm talking about a genuine dream, a vision that is beyond your experience today. The true purpose of a goal is to help you grow in your awareness of yourself. **What are your dreams? What are your aspirations? What are your goals?** You can begin thinking in a new and powerful way and begin discovering your true purpose in life.

Let your mind go and think carefully about what goal you wish to achieve. What is it you *really* want to achieve in your life? Write out exactly what you want on your goal card. Goals can be written down and, in our digital world, you can photograph what you have written down on your phone. You can even forgo paper by typing directly into your phone - reviewing those goals all the time. There are so many apps available to manage these goals in a fun manner, including countdowns.

You can keep the image of your goals as a screensaver on your phone and on your computer so you can refer to them often throughout the day - to get emotionally involved with them.

You could wander around an educational institution or business premises anywhere in the world and ask one student or employee after another what their goal was, and they would probably ask you what you meant.

If you find someone who has a clearly defined goal, ask if they have it in writing. Chances are that they do not. If you decide what you want and carry it with you, it must happen, it *absolutely* must happen. But you must think about your goal all the time and give everything you can to achieving it.

Why do we have goals?

The average person might have a goal to get more; to get higher grades, to get to their chosen college or university, to enjoy a dream holiday, to be the star of their sports team, to earn more money, get the next promotion or to be popular. **However, the real purpose of a goal is to grow.**

Having a clear goal causes you to draw something out of yourself that you did not even know was there. When you set a goal, you are going after something you want. If you already know how to reach it, it is probably a less exciting goal and you are going sideways and there is no growth attached to it.

Goals fall into three categories - A, B and C types.

A-Type Goals

A-type goals are goals you already know how to achieve. A student once asked if I could talk to him about his goal to do well in his exams - as he had done for the previous two years. I explained to him that doing well in his examinations was not necessarily a goal, because though he must absolutely focus on it, he knew how to do it. There was going to be no growth attached to it. He has already performed well in the examinations and he simply needs to repeat what he has achieved before: performing well in the examinations. Instead, a goal is something you go after that you have never done before. In his case that meant aiming to get straight-A exam results or to get into a top university, such as Oxford, Cambridge, Harvard or any other prestigious university, that he would not have not even contemplated before, or joining a world-famous company, or launching a new business venture.

B-Type Goals

When people move away from A-type goals, they generally go to B-type goals. Here, they gather all available information and resources and decide that if certain things happen, they can achieve a goal. They make a plan; if all these things happen then this is what they think they can do.

The A-type is what they know they can do. The B-type is what they think they can do. But there is no inspiration in going after something like that. If you are going to really accomplish something you have to be inspired. You have to pull on something that you have not pulled on before. It has to come from inside with a burning desire. People who go after B-type goals get bored and give up. Finally, the C-type goals are **about what you "really want".**

Many people say they do not know what they want, but in the majority of cases I am sure that they do. They may simply be shutting things down before giving them due consideration. To decide what you want, you have to sit down and relax and let your imagination wander. When you are going after wants, you are dealing with dreams and imagination.

C-Type Goals

The A-type goal is going after what you know, the B-type goal is what you think you can do and the C-type goal is your dream. We are conditioned to believe that dreaming is for children. Some schools even tell off children for daydreaming, which limits imagination. Dreaming alone will not bring you success and self-fulfilment, but it is a good starting point for the creative process.

Dreaming is for all of us. When our minds wander, our dreams unfold. Napoleon Hill said that the imagination is the most marvellous, miraculous, inconceivably powerful force the world has ever known.

The UK has some of the top schools, colleges, universities and companies in the world, but even those institutions have small creative departments. Everyone has the power to be creative, but the challenge is to go ahead and express that creativity.

Do not let anyone steal your dream. When you sit down to decide what you want, you will not know how you are going to get it; the fun is in finding out.

When I set a goal, if it doesn't scare me, I know I'm on the wrong track. So, if you know how you will do it, you are going sideways. Set a C-type goal that is big and beautiful and achieve self-fulfilment.

You must form a clear and definite mental picture of what you want. You can never achieve your goal or kick-start the creative power into action by sounding out vague desires.

You need to ask yourself *two questions* before you can achieve your goal: are you willing and are you able? We have got to build a dream. We take the dream and move it from a dream to a theory - take it and build an image. That is when we are giving our dream some serious consideration. We are starting to use our *reasoning* mind.

Before we can turn the theory into a goal, we must ask ourselves if we are able to do so. If we believe everything we have been taught by science and the laws of nature, we have deep reservoirs of talent, and infinite potential; so while we may not know how, we are able. The second question to ask ourselves is: are we willing to do whatever it takes to achieve our goal?

In that moment, a theory turns into a goal. As you get emotionally involved in the goal, you will find that your emotional involvement changes your behaviour and as your behaviour changes, your theory will turn into a fact. Once you reach your goal, it turns into a fact that puts you in a position to build bigger and better dreams.

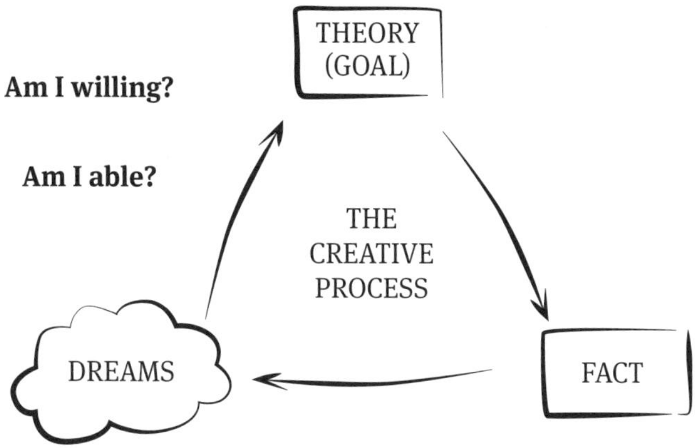

How do you decide what you want?

You sit down and start writing all your *wants* down; make a shopping list. Perhaps there are three goals that people should have – a personal goal, an educational goal and a business/professional goal.

Your personal goal might be to settle down and start a family; it might be to travel to a different country every year of your life; or to make a difference in your local community. You may even have a bucket list of things to achieve by the time you are a certain age.

Your educational goal could be to attain a certain result in your school or university examinations; it may be to learn to present ideas with confidence to an audience. It could be to study for and complete a master's degree or doctorate, or to learn to speak five languages fluently.

Your business and/or your professional goal could be a shared one where you might want to sit down with your peers or colleagues and consider what you could accomplish together.

It might be launching a new product or service for your business or conducting a piece of group research and publishing a complex paper on behalf of your organisation. It might be taking part in leadership programmes or charitable activities or supporting an innovative new business start-up idea. These are goals and, as we work towards them, we combine our energies.

When people are working towards something they love, they are alive. If they are just working, they have less fun. So, you have got to sit down and decide what you really want, and then you must start to make a list. You are capable of achieving anything and what you are really doing is raising your level of conscious awareness. The challenge of achieving success and self-fulfilment is not about achieving them; it is about setting out in our mind what we really want.

You are going to find that when you decide on the one thing on the list that you want more than anything, that will become the star you are shooting for. That is what you capture as your goal on your phone or your e-goal card or manual goal card. That becomes the goal.

It might be gaining a place at an elite university, getting top grades or a certain qualification, securing a job in a top company or winning a promotion that will enable you to lead the life you dream of. It could be an exciting gap year to explore the world that becomes your goal. Or setting up a new business. That is what you work towards.

Do not let another person dictate how you are going to live. And do not let conditions or circumstances dictate. It has nothing to do with what is going on outside of you; it is what is going on inside that achieves your results.

The late Stephen Hawking said that many people blame circumstances for where they are. Just think of how he defied the circumstances in his life. Aged just 21, he received the shocking diagnosis of motor neurone disease. At the time, doctors gave him a life expectancy of just two years.

Can you imagine being given such devastating news at the very peak of youth? All your hopes and dreams for the future totally smashed. No one would have blamed him if he had retreated into depression or given up on himself, just waiting to die. But he made up his mind to let the doctors look after his body, and he would look after his mind.

He refused to let it beat him; not to let the doctor's diagnosis define him, his education, his life or his goals. He lived for another 55 years to the astonishing age of 76. In fact this is the same age as my own mother, who lived a normal life.

He studied at Cambridge University, he became a world-famous physicist and cosmologist, he starred in films, he wrote best-selling books, he inspired millions. He married, had children, and left a legacy that will be remembered for all time. We are all capable of doing the same.

I have learned now, after studying this philosophy and the laws of nature, not to depend on external conditions and circumstance. The people who get on in this world are the people who get up and look for the circumstances they want, and if they cannot find them, they make them. So, you must absolutely refuse to let anything that is going on outside stop you.

We are goal-seeking individuals, every one of us. If you ever watch a baby, the baby's goal is to walk. Yet, the baby falls and hits its head – the baby cries, maybe bleeds, but it does not stay down. The baby gets up and is soon walking. Then, a few years later, that same child gets on a bike and the challenge is to balance and learn how to ride. Then comes swimming.

Think about your own goal and ask yourself what you really love to do. That is what you are going to get good at. That is what your purpose is going to be all about. That is what your goal is all about. Move towards what you want to do, have a personal goal, have an educational goal and a career goal, or indeed a life goal.

As the famous author, and my respected professor, Clayton M. Christensen once said: "How do you measure your life after achieving your goal?" Clay wrote a book about this topic and I would humbly urge you to study that wonderful book.

Your personal goal and your professional goal should be consistent with your long-term goal, which is your purpose. So, you want to make sure that as you work towards the big goal, all your little goals fall into place. I guarantee you will set something on fire inside of you. There's nothing like it! Goal achievers are productive individuals who are happy and have a self-fulfilled life.

Do not listen to people that tell you why something cannot be done. Ignore them, no matter who they are. Respect them but do not conform to their views. Those are just their views. **We are all unique and who can tell us what we want?** We have got to give ourselves a command and follow it – that is the discipline we need to learn.

Congratulations on taking your first step towards *Thinking into Character*. Now that you know a lot more about setting the right kind of goals, the next step is to act. Because that is where the learning really begins. Without action, goals are just dreams. Sit down and ask yourself: if I had all the resources required and there were no limitations, **what would I want to accomplish?** It's a great opportunity to be creative.

Think about yourself as a unique human being. Do not follow the masses. If you want to be free, become who you are, and not who your family members, teachers or employers want you to be. Become who you want to be.

"However difficult life may seem, there is always something you can do and succeed at. It matters that you don't just give up." Professor Stephen Hawking

CHAPTER 2

BRIDGING THE GAP

Now you have created your worthy goal and have an idea of what you want, you need to figure out the next step.

When we go through life without conscious awareness, we are literally programmed to act, think and behave in a certain way. Those habits become a part of our essence from a very early age. That is why most people are not doing what they really want to do. So, if you want to change your results, you need to think in a different way and change your habits. Habits are the 'cause' and results are the 'effect'. This is the basic law for creation, every 'cause' has its 'effects'.

This book is based on the success of many creative and successful people mastering human behaviour and potential. Through their experience and knowledge, I will illustrate for you a new way of thinking that will help you close the gap between what you **know** and what you **do**. You will be amazed at how different life looks when you start to change your habits - also known as **paradigms.**

PARADIGM

...is a mental program that has almost exclusive control over our habitual behaviour... almost all of our behaviour is habitual

Stephen Covey, in his great work, talks about the habits of successful people. You are on your way to understanding *you* a lot better; and when you open the door to new habits, results will begin to show – the results that you want.

This concept of the *Knowing-Doing* gap is, without question, one of the most valuable ideas that you will ever focus attention on.

There is a huge difference between what most people *know* and what they *do*. Our whole educational system is based on conditioning people to know more. We are given books, we study the books, the teacher or lecturer covers the contents in the books; and we are asked questions about the contents and information we have gathered and memorised.

If we remember the answers to the questions, and are able to describe, analyse, evaluate and provide a coherent conclusion, we get a grade and a qualification as long as we demonstrate how to get the 'marks' per the 'mark scheme' or assesment policy. The UK education system, particularly the exam-based approach of GCSEs and A-Levels, places a great emphasis on the ability to regurgitate information.

We could be an encyclopaedia of knowledge and yet not be very effective in creating results. Some of the most brilliant people in the world, who hold many qualifications, never make things happen.

However, for some reason, there are other individuals who may be functionally illiterate, or lack numeracy skills, or academic knowledge, but are so successful that they are multi-millionaires; building multinational organisations all over the globe.

Why does that happen? It is all to do with our **mind and our way of thinking**. There is a creative process that we need to be aware of. The mind is a marvellous tool. It has two parts – the conscious mind and the subconscious mind. The conscious mind is sometimes referred to as the *educated mind*, and the *subconscious min*d as the emotional mind. This is an important concept that we must all grasp.

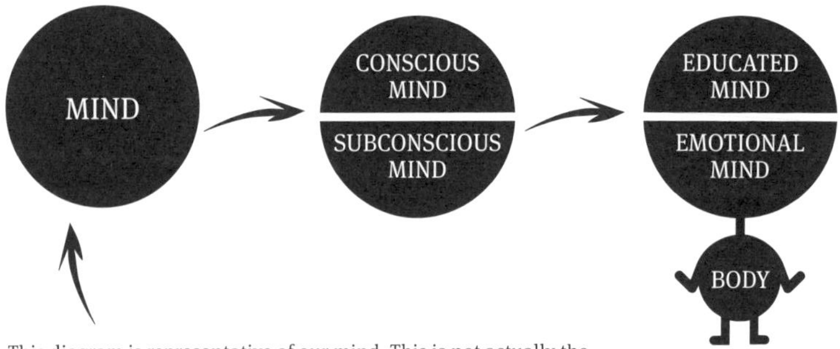

This diagram is representative of our mind. This is not actually the mind but we need a picture to visualise it.

The conscious part of the mind gathers information, and that is the part that schools focus on from an early age. As we reach adulthood, or even well into our adulthood, we go to university and build upon that knowledge. People gather information, but they do not necessarily do what they know how to do. As we age the gap widens because we know more but seem to do less.

Then we have the subconscious mind - the part of the mind that causes our body to do what it does. Essentially, it is our habits/behaviour and actions that determine our results.

If you do not go to the primary cause of results, there is not going to be any permanent change. So, you have to ask yourself why you behave as you do. That answer rests in your subconscious mind. It is in what we call the deep-rooted paradigm - a combination of habits inherited by genetics, and the environment we grew up in. The paradigm is that section in our subconscious mind that gathers habits.

School gave us valuable knowledge

However some of the SCHOOLS never taught us how to alter our **old PARADIGMS**

Therefore we frequently do not do, what we Already Know how to do!

Superior Information Overload and Inferior Results

Causes confusion and frustration

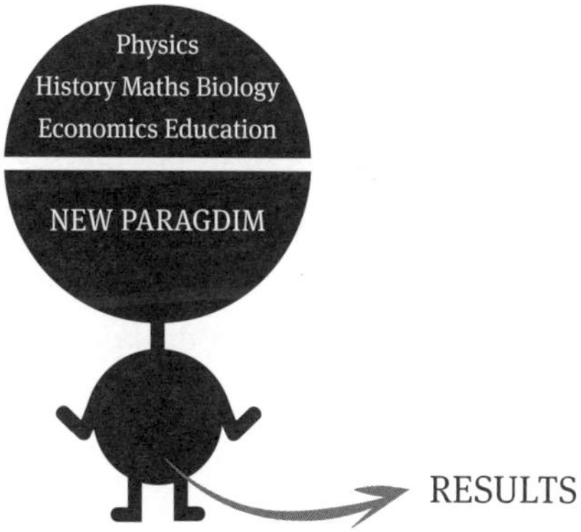

A habit is merely an idea fixed in the subconscious mind that causes someone to do something without any conscious awareness. The key concept to grasp is that *without conscious awareness* we are a kind of living dead. So we must ask ourselves how we can make it conscious.

We all have an enormous number of habits. When we get up in the morning, there is a routine that we move into and we automatically start doing things. Stop and consider your morning routine. You do not have a long think about brushing your teeth; you head to the bathroom automatically upon waking.

We do the same when we drive a car. Imagine passing your driving theory test and still not being able to drive a car. We study so many theories and we do not always bridge the gap of knowing and doing.

Stop and think of your classmates or work colleagues. Some of them regularly forget to bring their books or consistently turn up late for meetings. Their tutor or boss tells them off and has a chat with them about it. That individual is probably more organised for the next couple of days but the next thing you know they forget something again or come late, and they always have an excuse. It is a good excuse, but it is never the reason why. They are programmed to be disorganised and to come late.

There is somebody else who is always extremely organised and who is always totally prepared before they arrive at any meeting. That is part of their paradigm – they are always organised.

Let's think of all those aspiring authors out there. There are millions of would-be authors writing their first novels, all of whom set out with great determination to complete that project. Yet only a handful of people ever finish their book. Why?

Let's say you decide to start your first book, research paper or business plan – you have some great ideas, some intriguing characters and an amazing plot. This could be a bestseller! Or a world renowned product like the iPhone which changed the world. You start out with the best intentions. You know what you need to do to write your book or article. You need to spend at least an hour a day devoted to drafting your ideas. But after a few weeks you get distracted. You no longer wake up early to work on it. You are stuck on the same chapter for months; your mind wanders, and you have pretty much given up on ever completing your once-great idea. Sound familiar? It is very familiar to me.

Look at the author J K Rowling. At the time of writing her first Harry Potter novel, she was a single mother, on benefits and suffering from depression. Yet, she had a goal to write a children's book. She could have given up at any point and would have had good reason. Yet, she devoted her only available time, whilst her baby slept, to write. Instead of using that time to sleep herself, see friends or feel sorry for herself, she made a committed decision to do what she had to do to complete it. She devoted her free time to writing.

She did not give up. She knew what she had to do to get the book completed. Then, she sent her manuscript out to no less than 12 publishing houses, and they all rejected her novel. She could have felt rejected and given up. But she did not. Again, she knew what she had to do to be successful and despite the rejections, she continued to send it out until finally it was accepted by Bloomsbury.

The Harry Potter series has since become one of the best-selling book series in history and is the basis for a series of films and, more recently, spin-offs. J K Rowling progressed from living on benefits to becoming the world's first billionaire author. She did this by bridging the gap between knowing what she had to do and actually doing it. This was driven by her paradigms. She developed her skills to overcome any obstacles.

When a student comes to enrol with Regent or someone wants to join the Regent Group team, we ask a series of questions to find out how they are programmed. One of the first is about their greatest achievement so far. We want to get an insight into their history and see if there is a pattern to it, because if we start to understand the paradigm, we start to understand the power of habit. When we start to understand how the subconscious mind is programmed, we can start to change it.

Imagine a baby who is new to the world. Whatever is going on around the baby goes right into the baby's subconscious mind – all the ideas and thoughts. When the baby was born, they were already programmed – that's genetic conditioning.

Stop and think of this for a moment. You did not decide you like most of the food you eat; it was given to you before you had any conscious ability to decide whether you liked it or not. We are given food that our parents like – that is what we get. **Why do they like it?** Well, they were given food their parents liked. You have to go a long way back in your family history to find out who made the decision for you to do many of the things you are doing.

These habits are passed from one generation to the next, so when we are born, we are already programmed, which is why we look so much like our relatives. **Our body is an instrument of our mind.**

Environment is more important than heredity. The people we are surrounded by have more to do with who we are than, what is built into our genes at birth. The baby does not have any choice about the environment. It does not choose where it is born. It is just here, and it is being programmed.

That programming goes on for the first two or three years until the baby starts to consciously think for itself. But at that time, the programming is pretty well set. As energy flows to and through us, the thinking is already there. A person is programmed to think in a certain way. This paradigm is what causes us to behave as we do. We start at an early age gathering information. We gather more information and that information is loaded into the conscious mind.

However, rarely does a person do anywhere near what they know how to do. Your conscious mind makes decisions. We make decisions based on all kinds of different factors. But the things we decide do not always materialise.

We sit in our classes and meetings and we decide we are going to do things differently. We spend all kinds of time planning, but frequently our plans are not executed. That is because of paradigms. If we are insightful and honest about our paradigms and our behavioural patterns, we can appreciate the way we are programmed and accept that we will not change unless we change that programming.

Thinking by itself will not change results. You need to internalise the thinking through repetition and a change of habits. Then the paradigm is changed, the behaviour changes and the results change.

If we need to enhance our results, the only way to do this is to review our habits and change them to achieve the desired results.

I started from very modest beginnings. I had just £100 given to me by my late father when I fled the war and persecution in Sri Lanka. In 2000 we started our first private tuition lesson at Regent with just £20. We did not even have a name at that time. Regent Group is now a multi-million-pound, multinational company. I must confess that this Regent Group would not exist as it does today without my wonderful wife, business partner and friend, Tharshiny and many other team members who have been with us for many years. The staff team continues to grow, and they want to grow with Regent Group, not because they need to, but because they want to. I cannot underestimate their contribution. I also express my sincere gratitude to our Regent team.

I wanted to know how successful people are successful. I went to London Business School and then to Harvard and met Professor Clayton M. Christensen. He told me if I wanted to be successful with self-fulfilment, I would need to know who I was. I then studied Bob Proctor's teaching and spent a lot of time in the United States studying Earl Nightingale, Napoleon Hill and many other authors.

I am intrigued by how the world unfolds and how certain people can achieve exceptional things in their lives, regardless of a poor education or a difficult childhood - wanting to grow and always considering how to provide more service.

I was raised to believe that if you do not have a formal education you cannot win, and yet many successful businessmen and entrepreneurs do not have a good formal education, and they still win.

A lot of great entrepreneurs had issues with outside-in education. Among those without university degrees are Apple co-founder Steve Jobs and Virgin boss Richard Branson. Regent Group's vision is to bridge inside-out education with outside-in education. It is crucial we have both and then we can truly create a better world.

Branson says: "Looking back, I believe that the qualities that make for a great entrepreneur – such as boundless energy, a curious nature and, sometimes, an obstinate streak – are not often attributes demonstrated by top students in the classroom." So it should not be surprising that many of the world's great entrepreneurs and business leaders had difficulties with current formal outside-in education.

I am not saying that current formal outside-in education is not necessary. I am saying formal education needs to change and change is inevitable. We are here to make change happen and this is our chance to make a difference!

I also wanted to know what was happening to me. I was fortunate enough to have had a good formal education. Most people that are high performers at universities or in organisations are not understood by their peers or their superiors. **What do they do that is different?**

How come these thriving individuals are doing such a great job?

We look at people that are very high performers and ask how they do it. Some of them, society says, are not that bright, some of them have not gathered that much knowledge. But gathering the knowledge is not what gives them results.

I am not saying you do not need outside-in education because you do. Education is a basic human right. As the great physicist Albert Einstein once said: "Education is what remains after one has forgotten what one has learned at school." In essence, Einstein is referring to inside-out education remaining with humans. But we have to ask ourselves why people behave in the way they do. Think about the book-based knowledge that some of the people around you have. Then look at their performance and consider how they are closing the **Knowing-Doing** gap. That is what this is all about. The key is to balance outside-in education with inside-out education.

When you watch a person move, study them and you find that their behaviour is habitual. Start to understand that the factual knowledge they are holding in the educated mind or have gathered is not controlling what they are doing. Their paradigms are controlling what they are doing, which is in the emotional mind.

Listen to the conversations that are going on. Their tutor may call them into their office and to say their constant lateness to classes is not acceptable. Their boss may complain about their failure to arrive to meetings on time. They will say: "Tell me what I have to do, and I will change it." I know this because when I was younger, I myself was called into the headmaster's office and I promised that if I was given one more chance I would change. And I meant it.

I didn't change, because the tutor did not understand that it was my paradigm that was causing me to be late. I didn't understand it either. We had two unenlightened people trying to change and solve a problem and it was not going to happen. I was not doing what I was asked to do, what I said I would do, and it was my paradigm that was my problem. Paradigm is the problem in everything we do. The Knowing-Doing gap is miles apart. I still sometimes arrive late – it is my paradigm and I continue to work on it!

There are billions of pounds, dollars, euros, rupees and other currencies spent on training people to know more across the globe. But not on doing more.

How many times have you known what you should do but not actually done it? A new year begins and along with it comes your new resolutions and goals – to work harder, achieve better results, take up a new sport, eat more healthily, exercise more, read more, learn more. The list goes on, but you lapse within the first couple of weeks. We all start with great intentions and enthusiasm to improve ourselves but then fail to follow through.

How do we move beyond the Knowing-Doing gap? How do we turn that knowledge into measurable action?

We have to begin to focus on the paradigm. You need to understand why you are doing what you are doing and how to change it. When you do that, everything starts to change. The mind is something like a thermostat. It is set. It controls the temperature of our life and the way it is set dictates the results we are going to get. If we want to change the results, we have got to change the setting, or change the programming.

How? We remove some of the ideas that control the behaviour from the paradigm, replacing them with other ideas.

I trust that now you are starting to see the power of your mind and the effect that your thoughts have on your results. And not just the thoughts in your conscious mind, but more importantly the thoughts deep in your subconscious mind.

You are starting to learn about the role of paradigms in our personal, academic and professional lives, the understanding of which is critical to understanding why we all get so frustrated at times. It is because of the gap between what we know and what we do, and that gap is caused by unseen thoughts in our subconscious minds. If you are not getting the results you want, it is because your paradigms are controlling your behaviour. Change the paradigm, or habits, and that will change the results.

What is the gap between what you know you should do in a situation and what you are actually doing? What is your Knowing-Doing gap? Take time to consider this as it will guide you on why you do what you do and help you to alter your behaviour for the positive results you are looking for. It will take determination and soul-searching but give it a go. I promise it will be worth it.

Mahatma Gandhi said that by bridging the gap between what we do and what we are capable of doing, we would solve most of the world's problem. Most ailing organisations have developed a functional blindness to their own defects.

The Knowing-Doing gap exacerbates this problem. Stephen Covey calls this concept "focus and execution". Focus deals with what matters most - our goals. Execution deals with making it happen. To know and not to do is really not to know. The creation of success is underpinned by this profound truth. Execution is the great unaddressed issue in most organisations today. *Thinking into Character* enables organisations to learn the law of nature and achieve success.

I would also like to share the important message that I too am learning this habit on a daily basis and working to change my paradigms. It is a life long journey; it will take time, but one must be persistent and refuse to give up.

There are a multitude of people who consciously or unconsciously set the creative forces in action by the strength and persistence of their desires, but who remain poor or unsuccessful and are not able to achieve self-fulfilment because they do not provide for the reception of the thing they want when it comes.

By thought, the thing you want is brought to you. By action, you receive it. Whatever your action is to be, it is evident that you must act

NOW! There is never any time but now, and there never will be any time but now. If you are ever to be ready for the reception of what you want, you must begin NOW. Do not concern yourself with whether yesterday's work was well-performed or not, do today's work well.

CHAPTER 3

THE POWER OF YOUR MIND

By now, you should be deep into thinking about your mind and how it got you to where you are today.

In this chapter, I will explain how you can turn the habits that are holding you back into thoughts that will change your behaviour and create new paradigms, one habit at a time. I must confess, that I am also working on this, so we are all in the same position.

How do you know that your paradigms are not the right ones? Look at the results you are getting. **Are they positive? Are they really what you want?** If not, then open your mind and look at this powerful way of creating more favourable results.

I remember thinking that I had learned how to think when I qualified as a chartered management accountant in the UK and got my MBA. But I did not learn how to think this way, and I really wish I had learned when I was a child, but it is better late than never, so I am not late, you are not late, we all can learn every day. This is life long learning. *Thinking into Character* will get you on the right path quickly. You are on your way to getting what you want sooner rather than later. For me, the ideas were cemented when I was studying at Harvard Business School and working with Bob Proctor, the philosopher, teacher and mentor in the famous movie The Secret; and they expanded in my mid to late 40s. I have heartfelt gratitude for what I have learnt from these two learned gentlemen, Bob Proctor, Prof Clayton Christensen and all my teachers and various authors.

Are you ready to make a big change in your life? As you really understand what you are learning, you will change your life for the better. This is the chapter that will explain how to do all the things you have always wanted to do.

We have spoken a lot about paradigms. Paradigms literally control everything in our lives. Paradigms dictate our logic. A paradigm is a mental programme that has almost exclusive control over our habitual behaviour; almost all our behaviour is habitual.

When the Wright brothers introduced the world to the possibilities of their innovation - powered flight, they were the only ones who thought flying was a logical thing to do. Everybody else thought it was illogical, if not impossible.

Can you imagine a life without the internet, smartphones and gaming? Yet the internet was only conceived in the 1960s and commercialised in the 1990s. I recall my days at Prudential, my first job in 1993: no emails, just good old-fashioned paper memos and of course, faxes! Some of you were not even born; many of you will be too young to understand what a disruptive breakthrough this innovation was at the time. The irony is that the internet was always there, but we did not have the awareness to discover it. In this universe nothing is created or destroyed – we are simply not aware of what we have.

We have 3D printing now, invented by Chuck Hill. He was working for a small ultraviolet lamp-coating business when he suggested a new way to use the UV technology – to turn computer designs into working prototypes. They told him they did not have the time to try out his unbelievable ideas. Chuck Hill was finally given a little lab to play around in during his evenings and weekends.

He gave up his free time and worked relentlessly, believing in his vision even when others thought it impossible. After all, who would have imagined that anyone could invent a technology that can now literally print cars, human organs, human skin, bones or stem cells? A few years ago, this would have been considered illogical. But now the possibilities are endless.

Do you see how logic keeps us wired to where we are? As paradigms change, so logic will change.

I have watched students in our educational institutions go from failing grades to top grades by simply changing their paradigms. I have seen students change their paradigm of being disorganised by simply creating structured study plans and boosting their motivation by ticking off tasks as they are completed.

I have seen other students make paradigm shifts such as going from always being a silent observer in the classroom to asking questions on a regular basis. **How many of you passively sit in classes or meetings not engaging in the shared experience? Or not challenging your peers' opinions?**

It could be your paradigm not to speak out. Perhaps you grew up in a large family where siblings spoke for you. Perhaps you were once made fun of for asking a silly question and it stayed with you on a subconscious level. Your paradigm controls your thoughts and actions. Only by acknowledging that can you take the necessary steps to break the habits. Make a conscious effort every day to raise your hand, ask a question or share an experience. With enough repetition, that will become your new paradigm. What a difference it will make not only to your academic or professional life but to your personal life too, because you will be so happy.

It could also be something as straightforward as changing the paradigm of your sleep patterns. The relationship between sleeping and learning is an essential element of the learning process. When you are properly rested, your brain strengthens the knowledge you have learned during the day by assimilating information. The better you sleep, the better you learn.

Other students and our Regent leadership clients I have seen improve, have changed their paradigms to apply their learnings to real life. Learning is not about just studying for examinations, even though we have created a culture like this, it is about understanding knowledge, internalising that knowledge and understanding what to do with it. You can take ownership by consciously applying your core academic skills to real life situations.

Learning is where we consciously entertain an idea. We emotionalise the idea. We act on the idea and we observe a change in our results.

Think carefully about what paradigm shifts you can make to your life. You are capable of anything you set your mind to. My mentor Bob Proctor runs seminars addressing these issues in Los Angeles, and I believe everyone can gain a lot from them.

Let us go back and revisit paradigms. Remember, when you were born there was no conscious mind. It was just subconscious mind and whatever was going on around you went right into the subconscious mind and became fixed there. That is how you learn a language. We are literally programmed to speak the language we speak.

There are young children who can speak four to five languages. A baby does not have the ability to say: "I can't learn the language", so they learn it. Changing paradigms can also be compared to literally deleting the language we have learnt. Think about this concept of unlearning a language. We all know how we can learn a new language – through practice. Can we unlearn what we have learnt? *Thinking into Character* will assist you to **unlearn and relearn**.

It is fixed ideas that control our behaviour. We are literally programmed to live the way we are living. The question is, how can we change it?

Think of it this way: the paradigm controls the behaviour and the behaviour produces the results. Look at results in your life that you do not like. Let us suppose you are running a business and there is a negative with your cash flow, so you want to improve it. You might tell yourself that you cannot do better than the cash flow you are getting, because your customers simply do not want to buy more of your products and pay on time.

But your sales do not come *from* your customer; they come *through* your customer. Your sales come from you. When you change your behaviour, your sales can change too.

If your sales are not very good, I would like you to draw a minus sign on a piece of paper. Write down your sales the way they are now.

Now, take another sheet of paper and write down a positive sign. Write down how you would like your sales to be and write it in the present tense, for example: **"I am so happy and grateful now that my sales are hitting targets and improving profitability."**

Take the negative results and literally shred them — take great pleasure in ripping up the negative words on the paper, piece-by-piece. With each rip, imagine your negative sales figure is gone. Enjoy that experience. It is symbolic but it matters. Just do it – it is worth it.

Now look at the positive results in front of you. This is the part that is illogical. You have written out the positives of how you want things to be. You should write them out a hundred times. You can also make a recording of them and listen to them: "I'm so happy and grateful that my sales are hitting targets and my business is improving its profitability."

It is the repetition of the positive idea that eventually takes root in the subconscious mind. And as it gains strength, the negative idea that is already there becomes weaker. Pretty soon the one takes over and starts to control you and the other loses control.

However, if you think you are going to change just by doing this, forget it. You must realise your paradigm is a multitude of habits, and you can only successfully work on one or two habits at a time. Remember the language analogy, or about how you learned to drive and imagine now unlearning to drive or unlearning to swim or unlearning to ride a bicycle. Please give some serious thought to habits we have inherited by genes and by the environment.

Results can dramatically improve using this technique. In examples I have seen, the students only had to commit to a few things. Firstly they agreed to commit 30 minutes to studying the *Thinking into Character* programme daily and/or read this book. Secondly they created individual and group revision plans to manage their study time more effectively, helping themselves and each other. They worked on two or three things at a time and, because they worked as a group, there was a sense of camaraderie around changing paradigms. This concept will also work in change management projects in organisations.

It is with the repetition of ideas that paradigms change. The paradigm is a multitude of habits and ideas that is fixed in your subconscious mind. You may have inherited them at birth or picked them up during your childhood. It doesn't matter how you got them; the fact is they are there and embedded.

If you want to identify your paradigms, you need only observe your behaviour and results and you will see what is going on inside.

If you want to change a paradigm, you have to change it in the same way it was planted. There are only two ways to fix an idea in a person's subconscious mind; one is bang – just like that. It is like a shock and it is called an **emotional impact** – such as losing someone you love or being in a disaster of some kind. An emotional impact can cause a paradigm shift, perhaps making you re-evaluate your life and prompting you to make big changes.

Such events do not happen that often, and when they do, they are usually negative. It could be positive in the longer term, but the emotional impact is usually negative. I lost my dad in an unexpected event, which changed my life. Before my father's passing, I was always in the habit of putting on a watch when I got up. Yet his cremation was the last day that I ever did. My habit had changed as a result of an emotional trauma as my dad never ever wore a wrist watch in his entire life, so I cannot also wear one now, I have tried it many times since the incident in 2006, I put it on for a few days, then I cannot do it the way I did as a child. Now if I want to wear a watch, I have to force myself to make it a habit. I can still change it, but I have not decided to do so yet!

The other way to change a paradigm is by **constant spaced repetition (CSR)**; read the same thing, write the same thing, or listen and study the same thing over and over - maybe for a month or two, or over months and years. That defies logic and your logical mind says that does not make sense. But it makes sense when you understand how your mind works.

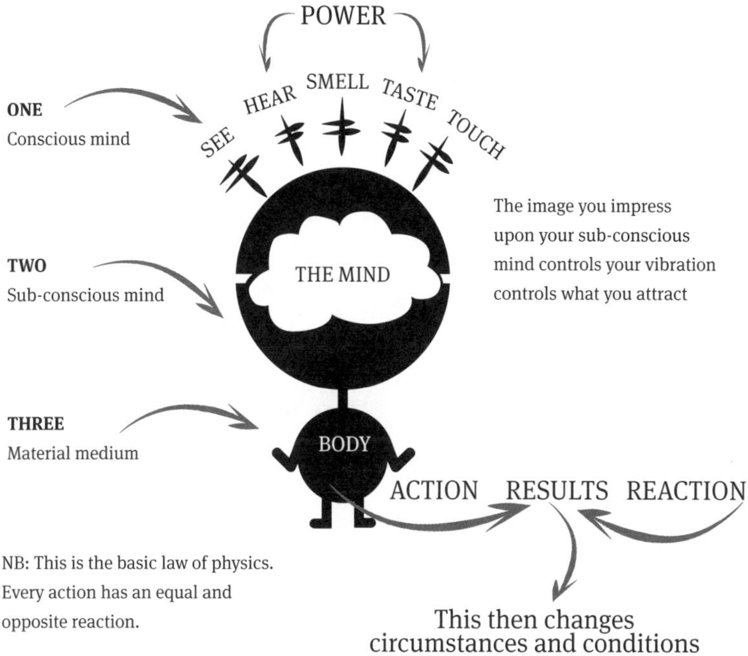

NB: This is the basic law of physics. Every action has an equal and opposite reaction.

WHY REPETITION IS NECESSARY

When Changing Paradigms

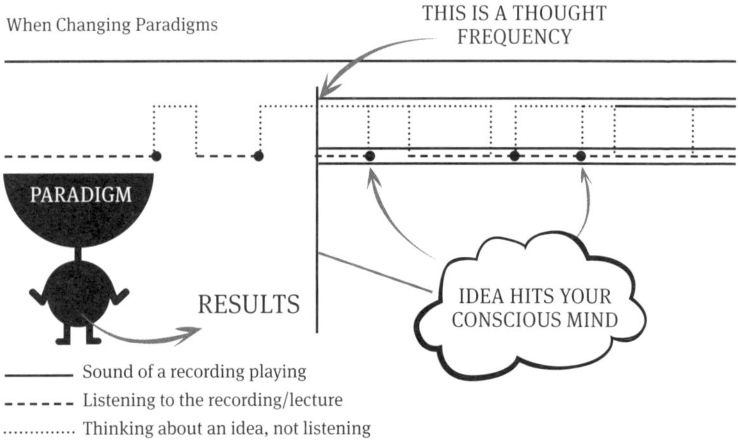

By constant spatial repetition we shift the paradigms.

Paradigms are nothing but a multitude of habits, and you can change them if you work on one or two at a time. If there is a group of you at your educational institution or place of work, it can help if you pick the same ones and work together.

As a group, make up your mind that you are going to come in 30 minutes earlier or wake up early and that you are going to study *Thinking into Character* from our Regent Virtual Campus or study this book. At first, you may not want to do that, but it is the only way to develop understanding.

You could arrive at your place of study or at your office or place of work half an hour earlier every day and re-read one of these chapters, or you could even get someone to read them aloud to you. If you do, I guarantee that within a year you will need a pair of binoculars to look back to see where you were. Your awareness is just going to continue to expand. This is the start of the proven methodology for the creation of success and self-fulfilment.

Change paradigms one or two at a time. By changing the paradigm, you change your results.

We do not have to put in longer hours, we do not have to work harder. But if we change some of our habitual ways of operating, we become much more effective. Successful people with self-fulfilment, have the awareness that they need to do certain things in a certain way, every day.

You will be amazed at the changes you can make, and you can have a lot of fun! You can turn it into fun because if it stops being fun, it starts becoming work. Love what you do, get excited about it, and get excited about making a change for the better.

For example, why not take the initiative to start a new club at your business? You could approach your boss and share your ideas for a new initiative that would be fun for yourself and your colleagues to join. Or join an existing club where membership or morale may be low and bring a positive attitude to it. Get involved. Give a new sport a chance. Start a research paper on an interesting topic and publish it on behalf of your educational institution. Kick-off a new project in your company. The possibilities are endless! One of my good friends and trusted advisers recently told me that, thanks to his own passion, they have started a car admirers' racing club at his institution, with a particular passion for Bentley cars. Their irony is that it is still to some extent private among members!

Let us make up our mind that we are going to change the way we operate, and we are going to enjoy it. We are going to get rid of the bad habits and replace them with good ones. We are going to agree one habit at a time and keep replacing them. We will be so much happier, and we will have more fun. You will see your whole world improve. When you change, you change everything in your life. Trust me, I know it works, but as I have mentioned before, I am still learning.

These chapters on paradigms are powerful, so dig into them. They are packed with tools that will help you get the results you want. You have learned how paradigms are the subconscious programmes that control our actions. **Every action has an equal and an opposite reaction.** The reaction will alter our condition and circumstances – we also call it the results.

Ideas come into our mind over-and-over to become fixed, so we are literally programmed to live the way we are living and to work the way we are working. The paradigm controls the behaviour without any conscious thought on our part and the behaviour leads to our results. Your results tell you what you are thinking at a deep emotional level.

Sort through those beliefs and paradigms that no longer serve you and change them to new beliefs that will serve you better. Spend as much time as you can on this and ask yourself about your habits and your deep-rooted beliefs. Challenge yourself about the things you do automatically and how your way of thinking is serving you. Ask why you are not getting the results you would like.

Once you start looking at your behaviour, you will be amazed at how much of it is unconscious, so have some fun. Break old habits, create new ones, and that will lead you to more positive results.

CHAPTER 4

THE STICK PERSON

I hope you can see that you have a major role to play in the way your life unfolds every day. We all have deep reservoirs of potential, but the challenge is to recognise that potential and maximise it. That has to do with how we think. Thoughts influence outputs, and whether we are thinking about solutions or problems can have a big impact.

I love this quote from Ralph Waldo Emerson, which has a special meaning for this chapter. He says: **"We become what we think about all day long."** It is your choice what you give your attention to and what you think about every day. Remember, you have control over your thoughts. Feed your mind what it needs to produce the outcomes that you most desire.

Now, I want you to think about who you really are. You may think this is a silly question and be thinking of your name. But you were not born with your name, and your name is just two or three words. It is not who you are. We look at people and label them with a name, but that is not them. Selva and Pankaj are just two words. I use those two words as my name throughout this book and in my life, but they are not *me*. In fact, this is not my full name, which is much longer, but it is what I am known by.

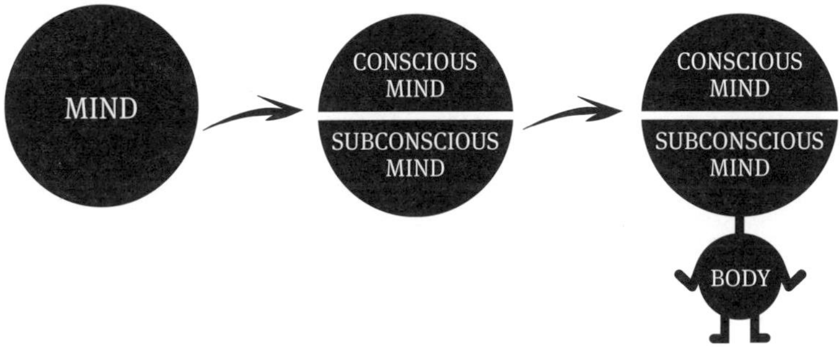

So, if that is not me, who am I? Am I my body?

You need to understand who you are. If you are going to change your character and the results in your life, you need to know who you are. You might not have been asked this before. You can go all the way through the educational system, and leave knowing little about yourself. You can gather information, but not know who you are.

I strongly suggest that you do more reading about the laws that govern us. Reading is key to learning. Research has found that a quarter of British adults have literacy levels so low they would struggle to read a bus timetable, and government figures indicate some 28 percent of UK adults are at literacy level 1 or below. That is because we hit that literacy level around age 12 to 15 and many of us never improve from that point on.

If this field is of interest, some key books to read are *Think and Grow Rich*, by Napoleon Hill; *The Science of Getting Rich* by Wallace D Wallis; and, *Lead the Field*, by Earl Nightingale. Although the titles may suggest the content is ‘getting rich’, these books look at how to be rich and fulfilled in both your personal and professional life. Reading them will absolutely enhance your learning and results. In this book I have summarised some of their key thoughts and ideas.

Reading was and is important to Elon Musk, the technology entrepreneur and driving force behind Tesla - it helped shape his early life. Musk was severely bullied throughout his childhood and even ended up in hospital after being beaten unconscious by some students in his class. He escaped through his reading. He read and taught himself computer programming at the age of 12 and sold the code of a video game he created called *Blastar* to a magazine called *PC and Office Technology* for $500. In later life, he was asked how he learned to build rockets and he simply said: “I read books!”

It is important to read the correct books to facilitate growth. Read a chapter of a book for 60 to 90 days until it is implanted in your subconscious mind. This may sound illogical but that is the only way to change paradigms. Our habits will change our actions. Actions will then create reactions as per the laws of nature.

Today, one percent of the world’s population earns more than 95 percent of all the wealth being earned. The average person has no concept of how to create wealth. We go through education and never learn that. You could have a degree in economics, banking or finance, but still not learn how to become successful with self-fulfilment or create wealth. We don't learn how to make decisions, which is why so many people are unclear about what they should do.

This comes back to not knowing who we are. When I came across this concept of inside-out education at Harvard Business School, I started reading a lot more, searching for the answer to that question. I started to study *Think and Grow Rich* and *Lead the Field*, and I kept reading them and trying the things the authors suggested. That is when everything started to change. I am so grateful that Bob Proctor helped me by explaining things in very simple terms. In turn, I am endeavouring to help others through writing this book.

When I set the goal of growing Regent Group, I wrote the goal on a sheet of paper and I read it as often as possible, getting emotionally involved every minute of my day. I also typed it on the Notes app in my phone. I wrote down that our company, Regent Group, was going to grow into a multi-million-pound, multinational company, and that drove me to focus. Now I use an app on my iPhone called 'e-goal' which my daughters introduced me to. It is really great.

You live on three simultaneous planes of understanding. You are a spiritual being (non-form), you have an intellect, and you live in a physical body (form). The mind is the greatest power in creation.

Now let us do some exercises…

First picture the door at No.10 Downing Street. What colour is it? What type of handle does it have? Can you see it in your mind? Of course you can and the image flashes in your mind as soon as someone asks you to describe the colour of the No.10 door. Now, imagine what colour the walls are in your bedroom? Can you see the colour clearly? Are there pictures on your wall? **Next, imagine what your mind looks like?**

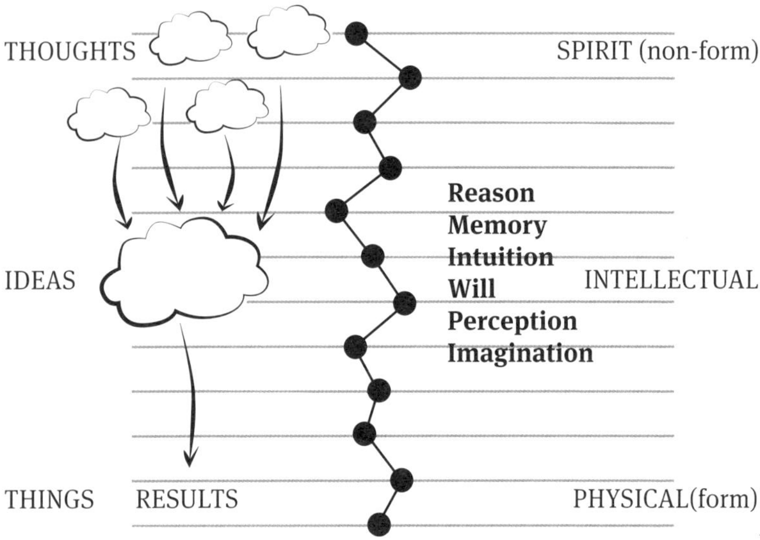

Lines are level of frequency. Each frequency is linked to one above and below.

Tough, isn't it? Are you thinking of your brain? Because if you are, your brain is not your mind any more than your little fingernail is. This is one of the big challenges in life. No one has ever seen the mind and yet it is the mind that must be changed if you are going to change results particularly the emotional mind which needs nurturing.

When I said to think of the No.10 Downing Street front door, a picture of the front door came to you. When I said to think of the walls in your room, a picture of your walls came up. But, when I asked you to think of your mind, **no picture came up.**

Dr Thurman Fleet, from Texas, USA, identified a problem in the 1930s. He said at the time we were treating the symptoms and not the causes of ill-health in the population. He argued that until the whole person was treated there was not going to be any improvement in health.

Today, we are still not treating the 'causes' of unsuccessful or unhappy people. We are not treating the causes of poor grades and underperformance. We are not treating the causes of youth unemployment or substance abuse, gaming addictions, teenage pregnancy, obesity or indeed – the biggest challenge of our time – mental health.

A recent mental health study shows that between 2005 and 2012 there was a 54 percent increase in the number of young people prescribed anti-depressants in the UK. This medication simply masks the symptoms of depression and do not treat the cause.

According to research published in 2018, more than one in five UK children are overweight or obese when they start school, and a further one in three children are overweight or obese when they leave primary school. They are being treated for diabetes, asthma, hypertension and heart disease but not for the cause of over-eating.

Another shocking fact is that one in four young adults in the UK is suffering from mental health issues. Depression and anxiety are the most commonly reported mental health ailments.

Of those who suffer
77 percent have depression-related problems,
74 percent have anxiety-related problems.

Additionally, **77 percent** of all students report that they have a fear of failure, with one in five saying this fear is prevalent in their day-to-day life. Yet, what is mental health? It is all about managing our marvellous mind.

Employability and career progression are huge concerns for young people. But most of the time, the status quo is accepted by employers, who assume the young employee is not capable of doing better, instead of digging into the paradigms and realising that he or she is programmed with low self-esteem, not believing they can do better and therefore not trying. If the employee understood his paradigms, he could change them, perhaps by committing to swap his border-line gaming addiction to focused overtime for two hours a day. His employers would soon notice!

Until we treat the primary cause of these issues, there will be no permanent change.

So, how do we solve this massive challenge?

We have to have a picture of the mind. Dr Fleet drew the stick person picture which is on the cover of this book and the next page in 1934 to illustrate the mind. It is just a couple of circles and a couple of lines, and we call this the **'stick person'**. Let the large circle represent the mind and the small circle represent the body.

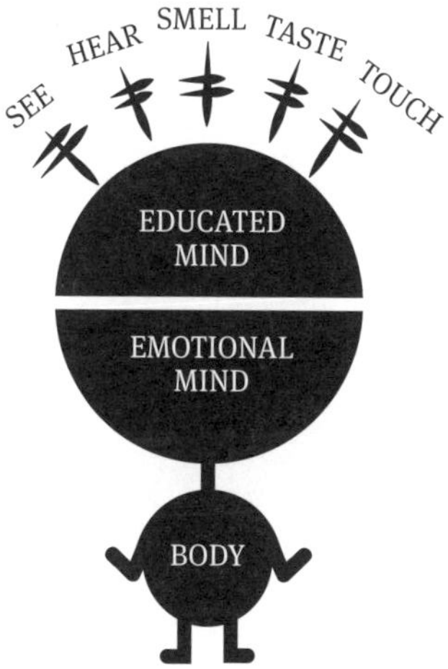

The mind controls the body and the body is an instrument of the mind. Think of the performance of people you know, or yourself. Some people, when they meet a stranger, are shy and pull back. Others are outgoing and have their hand out, asking all kinds of interesting questions.

Focus on this drawing again. Take that large circle and put a line right through the centre. Everything on the top half is referred to as the conscious mind and everything on the bottom half is regarded as the subconscious mind. The small circle at the bottom is the body.

Let your head represent the mind and everything from the neck down represent the body. That is not really the way it is, because the mind is in every cell of the body. But for the purpose of this exercise we need to work from a picture for illustrative purposes.

It is what is going on in the emotional mind that will determine what the body does. How do ideas get into the emotional mind? We put them there. There is a great power flowing to and through us and it never stops. As this power flows into the consciousness we have the ability to think. Mental activity is not thinking. Thinking is far deeper and linked with emotions.

The problem for many people is that they do not think. What surrounds the conscious mind are sensory factors. We can see, hear, smell, taste and touch and those sensory factors are what feeds information into our consciousness from the outside world.

We have been conditioned to live through these sensory factors and to go by what we see, hear, smell, taste and touch.

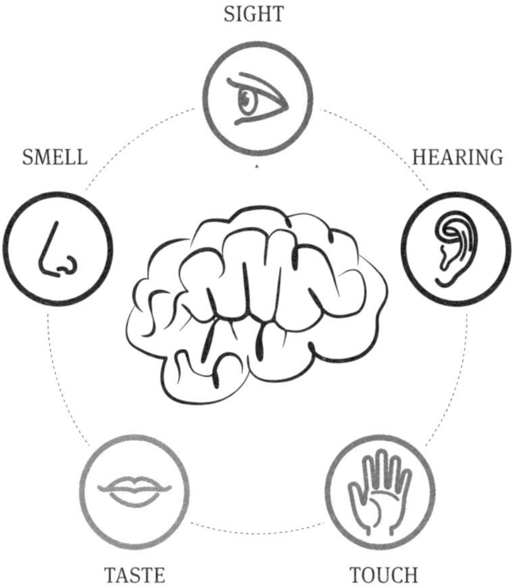

In school, we get a progress report that tells us what kind of student we are. We look at the report, our teacher looks at the report, and we take it home to our parents who use it to see what kind of student we are. At work, we are given a staff appraisal that sets out the judgements of our colleagues and superiors: We take that home and believe it tells us what we are capable of.

The truth is it does not tell us that. But that is the belief system we operate with. The report merely tells us where our mind was at for a few minutes, maybe a few weeks ago. It has absolutely nothing to do with potential, but that is what the employee believes. That is what the employer believes too, and we start believing in the comments in the appraisal. It becomes a self-fulfilling prophecy.

Think about the UK application system for higher education – The Universities and Colleges Admission Service, commonly referred to as UCAS, and the way in which predicted grades limit students, sometimes preventing them from applying for their dream universities. The system stifles aspirations, and that can in turn impact future careers and potential.

The report we get when we leave education dictates our job, our salary, our relationships, our life, just as the reference that we get from an employer influences our next role. We let those reports dictate what we are capable of. For instance, we may not continue with further or higher education even though we may be very capable of learning something more about a subject we are passionate about, because we believe in that report.

We may not apply for jobs that we are perfect for, because of the opinion of our last employer. We may end up in unhealthy relationships that are not worthy of us because of those opinions. And, if we allow them, suddenly they control everything we had dreamed of or hoped to do. In fact, reports and references just tell us what was going on in the past. They have absolutely no bearing on the future unless we let them, so we must not let them.

The stick person represents every one of us. As you start to understand how your mind operates and why you are doing what you are doing, I guarantee that your inner image will change, and it will change dramatically.

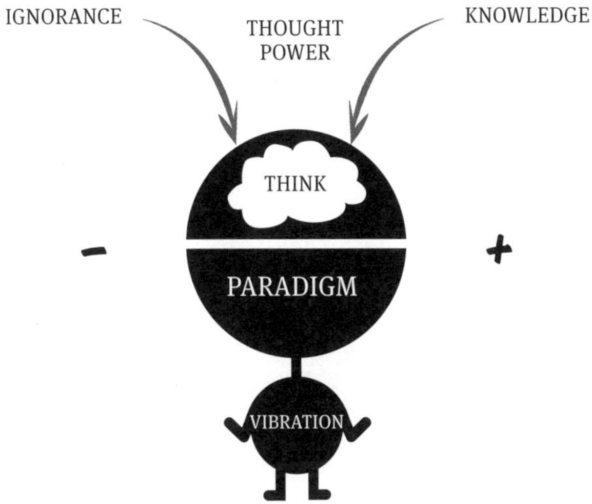

Let us pay close attention to the stick person created by Dr Fleet, because this is really how the creative process works. There is a power flowing into your consciousness. This is your thinking mind and where dreams are built. You take those dreams and you impress them upon your subconscious mind. This is what causes the feeling in your consciousness. *Feeling* is a word we invented: a conscious awareness of your thoughts and thinking. **This is how you get emotionally involved in the idea.**

Those emotions are then expressed with, and through, the body and that is what causes the body to change in a state of vibration. As the vibration changes, the action changes. And when your actions change, the universe reacts to that. It is action, reaction. The reaction alters your conditions, your circumstance and your environment or, as we say, your results. This is the law of nature: "Every action has its equal opposite reaction." It is basic physics, but still I only came to understand this fundamental theory recently.

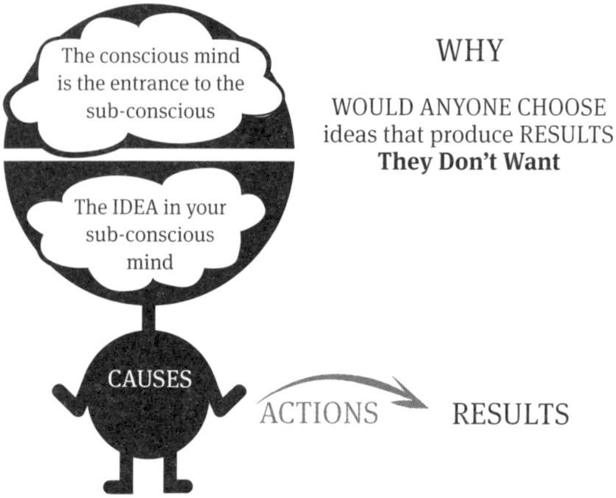

That is the process. Go through that several times – just keep playing it over-and-over, until it is printed on the screen of your mind. Then, when you find you are not feeling good, you know that you are emotionally involved with the wrong idea. Or, if you find the things coming into your life are not to your liking, ask yourself about your thinking, and the ideas your mind is getting emotionally involved with.

Let us explore this vital concept from the scientific and biological standpoint. Over 90 percent of our mental life is subconscious. The interaction of the conscious and subconscious mind requires a similar interaction between the corresponding nervous system.

The cerebrospinal, or voluntary, nervous system is the biological organ of the conscious mind. The sympathetic, or involuntary, nervous system is the biological organ of the subconscious mind.

The conscious mind is the channel through which living humans receive conscious perception by means of the five senses; seeing, hearing, smelling, tasting and touching. The system has its nervous system in the brain, and it is the channel of conscious mental action.

The involuntary nervous system has its centre in a ganglionic mass at the back of the stomach, known as the solar plexus - sometimes referred to as "the abdominal" brain. It is the channel of that mental action which unconsciously supports the vital functions of the human body.

The two nervous systems may work synchronously or separately.

The vagus nerve is one of the cranial nerves connecting the brain to the body and as such allows the brain to receive information about different areas of the body. From the cerebral region it passes onwards to the thorax, sending out branches to the heart and lungs. Finally it passes through the diaphragm, losing the outer coating that distinguish the nerves of the voluntary system, to become identified with the nerves of the involuntary nerve system.

In doing so it forms a connecting link between the two nervous systems, making the human a physical single entity.

A rather simple way of looking at the mental and physical interaction is to understand that when the *conscious mind* creates an idea, this induces a corresponding vibration in the voluntary nervous system. In turn, getting emotionally involved in the idea, causes a current to be generated in the involuntary system of nerves, which we refer to as the *subconscious mind.* This process instigates the *creative process.* This is how the *thought* becomes *results.*

Every thought entertained by the conscious mind and accepted as true, engages us emotionally; it is acknowledged by the brain – the switching station to the solar plexus and the part of the brain linked to our subconscious mind. Please remember that your mind exists in every cell of your body. This creative process enables the idea to be embodied in your flesh and brought to reality.

The subconscious mind works continuously for the general good, reflecting an innate principle of harmony behind all things. The subconscious mind has a life of its own, which is always moving towards harmony of the body/mind relationship.

To think correctly and scientifically, we must know the truth and laws of nature. To know the truth is to be in harmony with nature and the understanding of the subconscious mind, which is always fostering growth. As I have mentioned before, we are either growing or dying, but we have choice over our own actions.

***Thoughts* in the conscious mind, *feeling* in the subconscious mind, and *actions* in the body, whether through ignorance or intent, will result in *creation* or disintegration.**

Scientists inform us that we build a new body every eleven to twelve months on a continuous basis. So, we are really only eleven months old from a physical standpoint. Fittingly, we also celebrate the age of our body on an annual basis - our birthday.

If every time our body renews itself we build defects back into it via thoughts of fear, anger, jealousy or ill will, we have no-one to blame but ourselves. These thoughts destroy the nerves and glands bringing about mental and physical disease of all kinds. We are the sum total of our own thoughts; we have a choice to entertain, positive or negative thoughts and imagery. If we entertain positive thoughts we can create well-being at a mental and physical level.

The way to get rid of darkness is with light; the way to overpower cold is with warmth; the way to overcome the negative is to substitute it with good thoughts and imagery: Affirm the good, and the bad will vanish.

As you come to better understand this process, you can keep reflecting on your own life. You will know what is going on inside. You can always tell what is going on inside because of what is happening on the outside. That is your results. Results can be tangible and intangible: tangible results are monetary or physical achievements, while intangible results include satisfaction, happiness and well-being.

James Allen, a great Harvard professor, captures this concept perfectly in his book, *As a Man Thinketh*. He says: "We think in secret and it comes to pass. Environment is but our looking glass." In England we would call it a mirror. Whatever is going on in your outside world reflects what is going on in the inside world. You control the inside. Live from the inside out and stop living from the outside in.

As we proceed through this book, this stick person drawing becomes the "genie" as my mentor Bob Proctor likes to call it. You are going to understand why some of the most successful people in the world love this drawing. It has changed my life by helping me better understand myself and, because I understand me, I understand you to some extent, but I am still learning. This is an evolutionary process and it is lifelong learning.

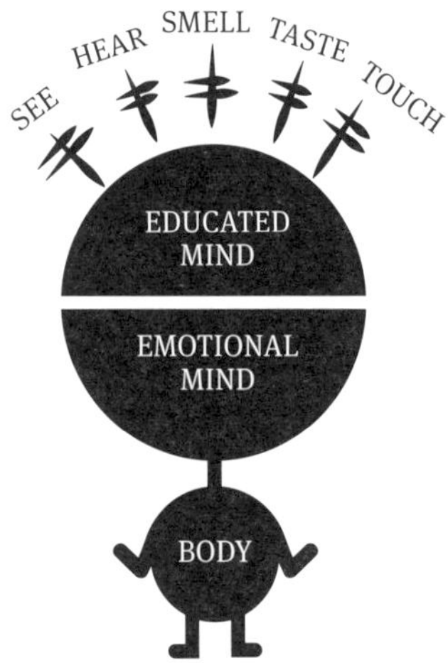

Everyone has a genius locked inside themselves that needs to be unleashed. That is what this stick person does. When you think of yourself, you can become very confused. But when you bring the stick person into play, you start to see the mind and the body; if this happens you will also understand it's because of what is going on in the subconscious mind. Changing the paradigms in your subconscious mind will change your behaviour into actions and therefore the results will change.

Mental activity does not constitute thinking. Those sensory factors are like five-lane motorways. There is information rushing into people's conscious and educated minds all the time; some of it seeps into the subconscious mind because very few people are focused.

I never understood this until I learned this material. Everyone told me that I should be focused, but no one gave me a tool to do this effectively. Carry on reading this book and you will master the skill of focusing, which will give you order in your life, the results you desire *and* enhance your character.

In the chapter on mental faculties later in the book, I will explain how to shut off those motorways, with all their information rushing in and causing confusion. This will help you to become focused, dedicated and disciplined. This is when your life will change.

Study the stick person and review this chapter over-and-over. Start to see yourself as the stick person and see everybody else as one. Then you can observe what they are doing and know what is going on in their mind. If you want to get others to change, you are going to have to help them to understand what is causing them to do what they are doing.

I promise you will keep getting more out of this chapter every time you come back to the stick person concept; it represents me, you and each and every human being. Let your results guide you. What is happening on the outside always tells you what is going on inside. Work from the inside out, as Prof Clayton M. Christensen at Harvard Business School explains when he talks about nurturing future leaders.

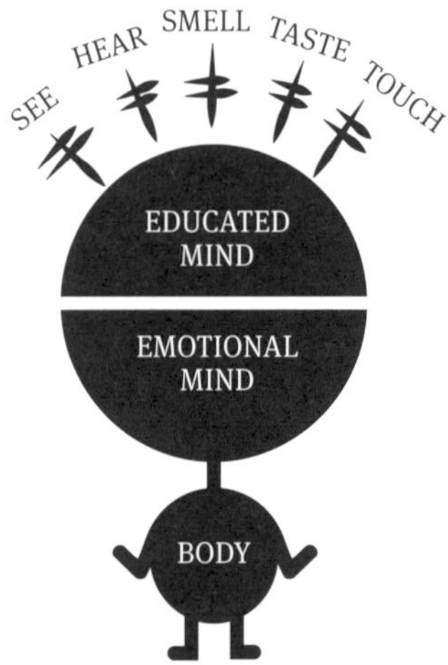

Bob Proctor once said, *"this is the most valuable thing I have ever learned".*

What are the goals that you set for yourself? Are you seeing them manifest in your world? Remember, you have control over the thoughts you think.

CHAPTER 5

MIRACLE OF YOUR MIND

You are going to start using a mind-altering toolbox that contains the secrets to mastering your life. You can no longer let external factors control your mind.

Remember that you are in charge of you. It really is that simple. You already have in your possession six mental tools which, if used properly, will help you create a world to your liking. They are right here in your mind, waiting to be activated.

They are:

- ***Perception***
- ***Will***
- ***Imagination***
- ***Memory***
- ***Reason***
- ***Intuition***

These tools and techniques will empower you to build your character and get the results you want. If you apply these techniques, your life will be transformed in ways you never imagined. You will look forward to going into your educational institution, place of work or any situation in life.

You will be stimulated and excited about your goals. You will be amazed at what you can achieve in life. It is like turning the lights on in a dark room – you will start to see things clearly. I now use these techniques on a daily basis, and I'm surprised at how powerful they are.

I will show you how to open your magic toolbox and introduce you to the tools you need to solve any challenge in your academic journey, your personal or professional life or achieve anything that you want to do in this life, as we only have a single chance, in our respective opportunity to live in this world, to make it worthwhile and make it what we want.

In previous chapters, I introduced you to sensory factors. They are like little antennae sticking out of our conscious mind. We see, hear, smell, taste and touch – and that is how we are programmed. We are programmed to pay attention to what is going on outside and we live from the outside in. You will never, ever do anything of any meaning if you are living that way.

Napoleon Hill said: "An educated person is not necessarily a person with an abundance of general or specialised knowledge. An educated person is a person who has so developed the faculties of their mind that they can acquire anything they want without violating the rights of others."

Most people are not even aware of what their conscious faculties – their mental muscles, are and yet they are extraordinary mental tools. Let's look at them one by one.

Perception

Perception is the intuitive recognition or interpretation of sensory stimuli, related to all your senses. Imagine I am having coffee with a friend at an outdoor café. A bumblebee suddenly appears and hovers over our table. I smile as I see a beautiful sign of nature and a realisation that spring has finally arrived. My friend sees a terrifying insect and jumps up shouting, running for shelter. We both see the exact same thing, but we each have a totally different perception of it. Who is right and who is wrong?

You may remember in 2015 a picture of a dress circulated like wildfire on the internet with people divided as to whether the stripy dress was gold and white, or blue and black. Who was right? The answer was that everyone was right. It all boiled down to the rods and cones in our retinas and how they perceive colour.

The crucial concept is that just because one of us is right does not mean the other is wrong. We have a perception problem. There are many ways of looking at everything and our perception is our own point of view. If we can see things from another point of view, we may be able to achieve things we did not previously think possible. Perception is a marvellous tool for appreciating the power of seeing things differently.

Will

Then we have Will. The will is the faculty of the mind that selects, at the moment of decision, the strongest thought or desire from among the various thoughts or desires present. Will does not refer to any particular thought, but rather to the mechanism for choosing from among one's thoughts.

The will gives you the ability to hold one picture on the screen of your mind to the exclusion of all others. Remember that our sensory factors are like five-lane motorways, with information flying into our consciousness. We hear noises, see lights, pick up smells, and all of that comes into our consciousness as a muddle of unrelated information.

We have to stop this rush of information causing confusion, and we can do that through the use of will. Our will gives us the ability to focus and concentrate, so it is another powerful tool.

Think of the will and concentration that spinal surgeons have. A surgeon can do an almost perfect job, but one little slip could paralyse the patient. There are no second chances.

Mr Bob Chatterjee, a famous UK spinal surgeon, talks about presenting one personality to his patients and then shifting into another of intense concentration before surgery.

He says: "Before an operation, I need to put patients at ease. They don't want to see a pumped-up surgeon. They are trusting someone to go into their spine and not paralyse them."

But once the patient is unconscious, he shifts into operation mode: "I sit down and go through the plan," he continues, "It helps focus the mind. Most operations last around five hours, but some are longer. Once, I was in surgery for 36 hours straight operating on a man who had dived into a shallow river."

Imagine the amount of will and concentration required for such lengthy surgery. One wrong move could result in paralysis or death.

Practise developing your will with the following exercise. Take a pencil and put a little dot on a wall opposite your favourite chair and when you are sitting there just stare at the dot until you and the dot become one. Every time you are by yourself and there is nothing else going on, totally relax and try it, with no background noise.

At first, you might only be able to concentrate for a millisecond, but it will get longer and longer. You are strengthening your will. When you learn to concentrate on one thing, you can learn to concentrate on anything.

Imagination

Next comes Imagination. The imagination is the most marvellous, miraculous, inconceivably powerful force the world has ever known. Napoleon Hill said that and I have adopted it and believe it.

Everything is built through the imagination. Buildings, vehicles, the most advanced computer technology; they are all nothing but the manifestation of someone's imagination. To go a step further, consider how everything is created twice, first in the mind and then in the outside world. You have got an imagination, so use it constructively. Use your imagination to see how you can do much better than you are doing.

Author J K Rowling says: "We do not need magic to transform our world. We carry all the power we need inside ourselves already. We have the power to imagine better."

Memory

The fourth mental tool is Memory. There is no such thing as a bad memory – only weak memories and strong memories. Anyone can develop a great memory, and there are techniques you can learn to better remember names and numbers. The way you remember numbers is not the way you remember names, but both can be improved. If you need to improve your memory, take the time to research techniques, study them and work hard – there are some great books available to provide support.

You might take inspiration from Ben Pridmore of Nottinghamshire, UK, who in 2019 holds the world record as the first man to remember a randomly shuffled pack of cards in under 30 seconds. He also holds the title for remembering 28 decks of 1,456 cards in just one hour, and he can recall 4,140 digits of binary numbers – a string of numbers consisting of just two characters, 1 and 0.

Reason

Next comes Reason. It is reason that gives us the ability to think. Thinking is the highest function we are capable of, and we can be taught how to think in just the same way as we can be taught how to type or play a piano. We should devote time to learning how to think, because that is how we tap into infinite possibilities and build ideas.

An idea is nothing but a thought or a collection of thoughts directed towards a purpose. Let us think and grow into new dimensions. Let us think how we can do what we are not doing. Let us think how we can do better. Let us not spend any more time on negatives, thinking why we cannot do things. Instead, build the image of what you want; use your thoughts to cause new feelings and those feelings to cause better actions - those actions to produce a new result.

When you react to what is going on around you, whether that is a condition, a circumstance or a person, you let that control you. Instead, you need to respond and maintain control. You need to use your thoughts to stay in control of you, and that is the power of reason.

Intuition

Finally, we come to Intuition, which is the mental tool that gives us the ability to understand something instinctively, without the need for conscious reasoning or evidence. Intuition was built into humans to ensure the survival of our species in the face of danger. It was hugely important that our ancient ancestors could *sense* danger when they could not necessarily see it.

Intuition has evolved considerably since those times and is now often referred to as "gut instinct". Think about how you get a *feeling* that something or someone is wrong or right. Have you ever felt that someone is following you or watching you before you have seen them? Or have you known who was calling before you even picked up the phone.

Steve Jobs famously said: "Have the courage to follow your heart and intuition. They somehow know what you want to become."

There is a ray of energy around your body and you can pick up the energy coming from another person through your intuitive factor. Get tuned in. Start developing your mental faculties. You will become a much more powerful human being – you will be more creative and achieve better results.

PERCEPTION WILL IMAGINATION MEMORY REASON INTUITION

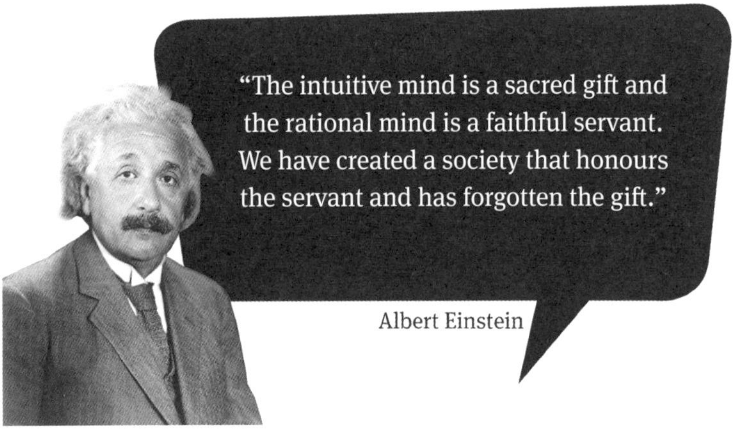

We have learned how important it is not to underestimate the miraculous mental tools that we all have at our disposal. These tools are not necessarily taught in school or university, but they should be, because they are key to getting the results that you want. The more you use these tools, the better they can help you.

The technological revolution has only just begun to permeate our everyday life. As time passes, artificial intelligence (AI) will become ever more sophisticated. However, AI's limitations are revealed in decision that requires lateral thinking, imagination, intuition and reasoning. Those mental tools, which schools have so far failed to develop, are needed now more than ever as computers can easily replace much of the work humans have always done with an educated mind.

Inside-out education is all about developing the emotional mind. The march of artificial intelligence will not stop. It presents threats, but it also brings countless opportunities. Humans, and all their mental faculties, will become ever more important in the creation of success. We just have to be smarter than a robot and the only way to achieve that is to understand the power of the subconscious mind, and indeed develop those valuable mental faculties.

Look at a challenge you face and consider how you would like to change the situation. Then commit to taking actions and using these tools.

CHAPTER 6

YOUR SELF-IMAGE

I am going to introduce this chapter with a quote from Dr Maxwell Maltz, a cosmetic surgeon and the author of the bestselling book *Psycho-Cybernetics*. He said: "Self-image sets the boundaries of individual accomplishment." In this chapter we are going to think about the image that we have of ourselves and how that influences every part of our lives.

Self-image controls the way you speak, look, love, dream – everything! If you have a negative image of yourself, your results will be negative. If you have a limited image of yourself, your results will be limited. But you *can* change your image and change your life. You are now going to learn how to write the script of you, with a new self-image. If you already have a positive image of yourself, this chapter will improve it still further.

A crisis of negative self-image affects many people in the UK. A 2014 study found that more than 60 percent of us admit to having a lack of self-confidence that prevents us from participating in certain activities, and not just sports. Insecurities prevent students from putting their hand up in class, hinder job applicants from attending interviews, stop business leaders approaching potential new clients, affect relationships and encourage people to retreat into a shell, or to inhabit a social media world where bullying is rife.

It is not enough to send young people off into the world with a clutch of good A-levels, undergraduate or postgraduate degrees. They need to be confident enough to look up and embrace all life has to offer. So often during job interviews I see candidates with great qualifications hunched over, looking down and struggling to make eye contact.

Think about what you want to be and what kind of life and career you see ahead. Ask yourself what is holding you back, and you might find it is your self-image.

I learned to create a script for myself recently when I realised, I had to start thinking "star", instead of "supporting player". I vividly remember sitting down to write the story of my life as if it was already happening.

I put my screenplay in a safe place and read it every chance I got. Then, one day, I decided to make it happen. I started investing more in myself, learning who I really was, my purpose and what I was capable of. When I look back on that journal entry now, so many of my dreams are now my reality.

Dr Maltz wrote *Psycho-Cybernetics* in the 1960s – psyche being Greek for 'mind' and cybernetics being the science of control and communication. The book discussed the control mechanism in our minds that determines what comes into our lives and how well we do. We refer to it as our self-image.

Dr Maltz was performing cosmetic surgery on people who may have had a crooked nose or scarring on their face. He would rebuild their nose or remove the scar, but he noticed that in addition to the difference in the person's appearance, there was also often a great psychological change. They not only looked different, they felt and acted different too.

But, he said, this was not always the case. Sometimes, regardless of how successful the physical operation was, there was no psychological change. This led him to conclude that we have two images; one that we project to the world, which is the way we dress, walk, talk and comb our hair. The other is our own internal image of ourselves.

The picture that we hold on the inside shows on the outside. If we have a negative or a bad self-image, our results reflect that.

Our self-image is passed along in our genes and developed to a large extent during our childhood. A child raised with praise grows up to be a confident adult. A child raised with criticism often grows up to be insecure.

Confident individuals understand who they are and the power of their mind. They understand something of and like themselves. And yet even hugely successful people can have poor self-image issues.

The fashion designer and former Spice Girl, Victoria Beckham has spoken about how she has never believed that people are interested in her, and often feels the need to prove herself: "When I was on stage with the Spice Girls, I thought people were there to see the other four and not me," she said. "And when I go out with David and people take pictures, I think they are there to take David's picture. It was never my intention to prove anybody wrong. I wanted to prove to myself that I could do it. I don't have to work; I need to work."

Dame Emma Thompson DBE, one of Britain's most acclaimed Oscar-winning actresses, has said she has a voice in her head that often puts her down: "I have a fantastically loud and mostly punitive voice in my head that says, 'you are not good enough, you stink'," she says.

The people who do not understand themselves, who are super-critical and who feel inferior, have a poor self-image. But I believe we can change our self-image if we do not like it.

At the centre of your consciousness is an image of perfection. We have amazing creative faculties, but they can be buried in false concepts, so it is only on rare occasions that our perfection sees the light of day. It is our responsibility to get rid of those paradigms and insecurities so that the perfection shines through.

How do we do this? Well, the more you study you, the better the image you are going to have of yourself. And that image is vitally important. It operates much like a thermostat in a room controlling the temperature, or like the automatic pilot keeping a plan on course.

Imagine a teenager who goes on a diet in the belief they are overweight. Their subconscious mind is programmed to focus on whatever weight is lost. They lose ten pounds, but unless they address their self-image, they will put it back on. It is another example of a paradigm that needs to be shifted.

Consider a student who is averaging a B grade. Imagine their grades drop to C grades for one month – the following month they will probably go right back up again. The same if they achieve A grades for a month; they will go back down.

The image you hold of yourself literally controls your life. When Dr Maltz came up with this idea it was considered the greatest psychological discovery of a generation. All kinds of lives were changed as a result of that book: you might consider reading it.

The question is, how can you change your own self-image? First, you must understand that you hold an image in your subconscious mind. You must then put you conscious mind to work and deliberately choose the kind of person you want to be by addressing that image. You must decide what you really want to be like.

I generally pick people I know that have qualities I really admire. I aspire to their particular character trait and picture myself being that way. In fact, I often follow entrepreneur Richard Branson, because I admire his can-do spirit. One of my favourite Branson quotes is: “If someone offers you an amazing opportunity and you are not sure you can do it, say yes – then learn how to do it later.” I incorporate that attitude into my daily life and build it into my self-image.

So, sit down and write out a new description in the present tense.

Then totally relax and start to see yourself as that person. This *imagined reality* is an actor's technique - something that allows you to literally become that person.

Watch films. I often watch the movie *Steve Jobs* - one of my favourite films, starring Michael Fassbender as Steve Jobs. Fassbender acknowledged his lack of physical resemblance to Jobs but said he was more interested in capturing Jobs' essence than in his appearance. He also said he aimed to depict Jobs as "somebody who was passionate about his vision".

His acting was incredible and as you watch it, you realise he took a script, read it, re-read it, memorised it, internalised it, and ultimately became the script. Despite his lack of physical resemblance, he became Jobs in the movie, and that is what you want to do – be the star of your own movie, but in the real world.

Most people are *extras* in their own movie. They see other people and they think those others are the stars and they are just in the supporting cast. Resolve to make yourself the star of your film. Sit down, build the picture and then totally relax to allow yourself to become that person. Do that often – maybe a few times a day. It only takes a few minutes.

Try reading Stella Adler's amazing book, *The Art of Acting*. Stella Adler was one of the greatest acting teachers in the world before she died in 1992. She taught Marlon Brando, who wrote the foreword in her book, and she was widely revered.

Look again at Emma Thompson, who said: "I am an instinctive actress. I don't have a technique because I never learned any. I do the cerebral bit before I start. Then I just let it be. I allow whatever rises to rise naturally. You are tricking your subconscious. I work from the inside out."

There is a science of control and communication locked up within you, which is your self-image. That image that you hold of you controls how you walk, how you talk, and how you meet and greet the world. Build a better image and see yourself as everything you are supposed to be.

There is something wonderful about you. Get in touch with it. Hold that picture. Become that person. I am not talking about conceit, but a healthy conscious awareness of who and what you are. Be good to yourself because if you are not, no one else will be.

You have creative faculties. You have creative potential. There is a power flowing to and through you. You need to work towards one objective and make it happen.

Now make sure you truly understand this, because if you do not, you will not be able to achieve it. Bob Proctor always says that you do not understand anything until you can explain it to someone else so that they understand it.

You can accomplish a lot in a short period of time, and you can have a lot more fun.

Think about the image that you have of yourself, and whether you are happy with what you see. Remember, every person has a self-image and it is reflected in their results. If you want better results, check the image you have of yourself and begin to make a change.

CHAPTER 7

BREAKING THE TERROR BARRIER

When you embark upon the pursuit of your goals, the landscape may be riddled with obstacles that get in your way, and one of the biggest barriers is fear. We can refer to this as the *terror barrier*, as explained by Bob Proctor, and it is easy to discover your terror barrier if you set a goal outside your comfort zone. Once you become emotionally involved with the goal and you start moving towards it, you can crash right into that terror barrier and it does not feel good.

Let us be clear, fear can be helpful at times. Fear is the mind's way of telling us that danger or adversity lies ahead. But fear can also wreak havoc, because it can hinder imagination and choke ambition. At its most devious, it can make every obstacle seem impossible to overcome. Consider the German proverb "Fear makes the wolf much bigger than he really is."

The trick, of course, is learning to overcome our fear so that we see the wolf as just a wolf. But that is not easy. The terror barrier might be keeping you from the results you desire. It could explain why so many people get excited about a goal but give up along the way, and why only a small number of people achieve their ambitions.

The truth is, most people do not hit their goal because they set the wrong one. You have to go after the big one. As Richard Branson says: "If your dreams don't scare you, they are too small."

But be aware that you are going to come face-to-face, at some point, with your terror barrier. It could sink you, but if you build an understanding of what is happening, you can crash right through it. Everyone that has ever accomplished anything has come up against their own terror barrier and got through it.

To understand this, we have to go back to the stick person concept. Bob Proctor explains this important idea using four stages of ***Bondage***, ***Reason***, ***Conflict*** and – beyond the terror barrier – ***Freedom.***

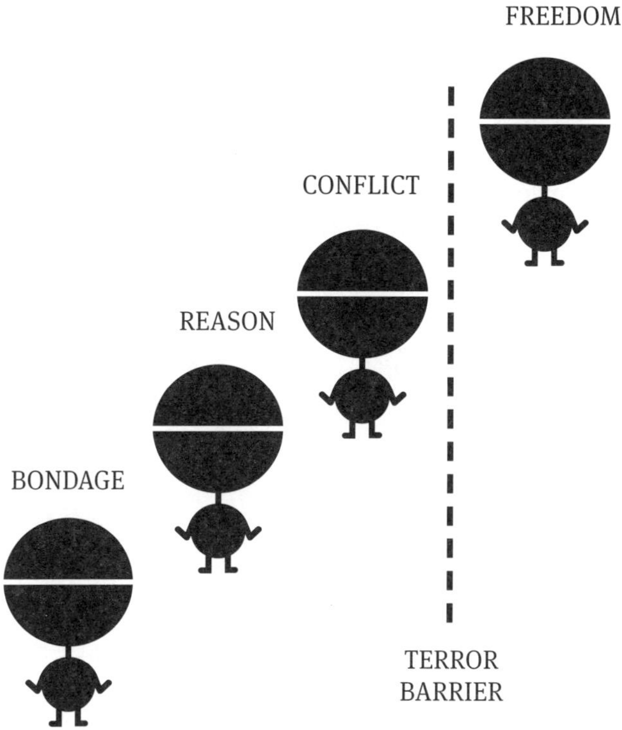

In the ***Bondage*** phase of development, an individual is exhibiting what is referred to as X-type behaviour, where X is the unknown factor. They do not know what they are trying to achieve, and they achieve X-type results as a consequence.

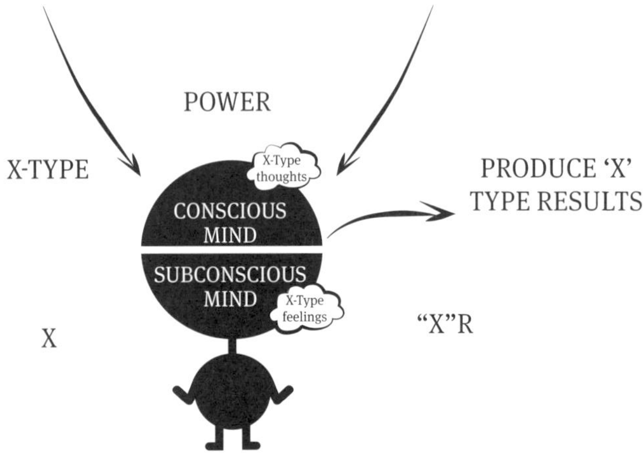

Students that achieve C-grades every year are not thinking with purpose in the same way that a student achieving A-grades thinks. They often barely even dream about results. X-type conditioning produces X-type thoughts and students keep getting the same results year in, year out. Those individuals are living in *bondage*; they are not free. They do not even understand the concept of freedom.

Next, we move from bondage to ***Reason***. That same student begins to entertain a Y-idea, which comes from somewhere else. As long as the Y-idea is just in the conscious mind, nothing happens. The Y-idea is a goal that is way out there, and this person with the X-type conditioning, X-type behaviour and X-type results begins to entertain the idea of doing something greater than they are currently doing. They start to aspire to greater things.

What is really happening is that the uniqueness within them is seeking expression, so they begin to think beyond where they are. This is what we call *reason*. You can think anything you want, but if you do not internalise it, nothing happens.

Then we go to the next level, and we hit the *terror barrier*. Now here is a person with a Y-idea in their conscious mind, and they start to get emotionally involved in the Y-idea. When they get emotionally involved, they are in an X-Y vibration. This is chaotic, and instantly worry and doubt registers on the conscious mind and fear on the subconscious mind. On a physical level, there is anxiety. They hit this terror barrier and they bounce right back into bondage – that is what happens with almost everyone.

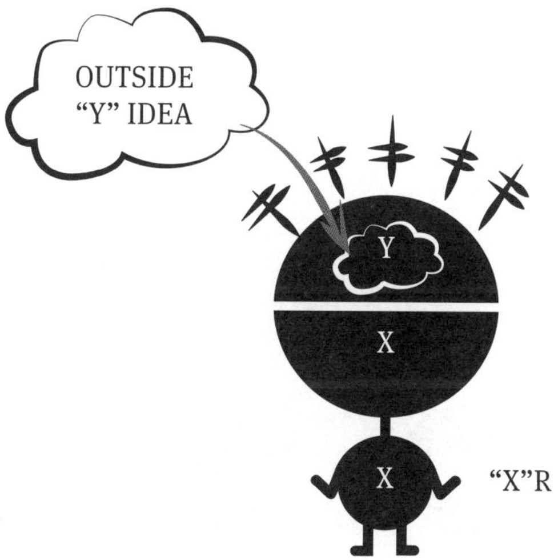

A person who wants to start his first business has an innovative idea, has done some market research and believes it is a great idea. But then the terror barrier hits… he keeps waking up in the middle of the night absolutely terrified and cannot get back to sleep. What if his idea is not good enough? What if the economy takes a downturn? What if he runs out of cash to fund it? He has the great idea and wants to launch the business, but he is scared. So he drops the idea.

A student has worked hard, finishes their education and sees their dream job advertised. They want to apply for it but are scared. This job is perfect in every way and they are newly qualified; but have absolutely no experience. This role is just what they want and have always dreamed of, but they are scared that other candidates will have more experience. They are scared of failure. So they don't apply, or even if they apply with *fear* they do not succeed, they invite failure.

Fear strikes: "What if I fail at the interview and I do not get the job?" When you get involved in the X-Y vibration on an emotional level, your whole being changes. That is the terror barrier.

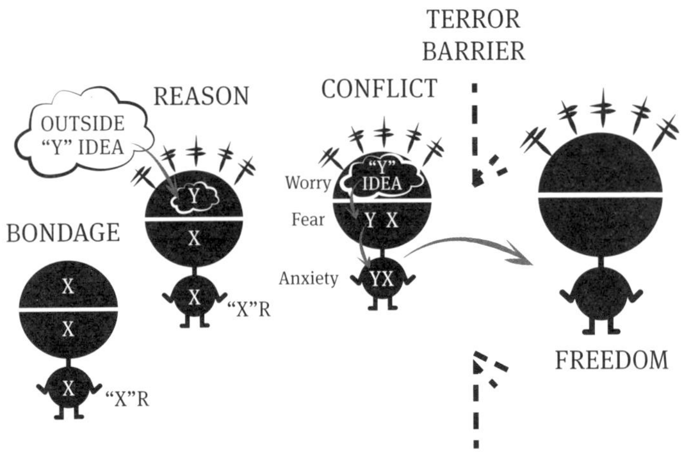

Look at Michael Jordan, famous for being cut from his high school basketball team. He turned out to be the greatest basketball player of all time because he never let fear of failure deter him. I love this quote from him: "I have missed more than 9,000 shots in my career. I have lost almost 300 games. On 26 occasions I have been entrusted to take the game-winning shot, and I have missed. I have failed over-and-over and over again in my life. And that is why I succeed."

Elon Musk says: "Failure is an option here. If things are not failing, you are not innovating enough." Think about that. You only truly fail when you do not try.

This is the same for us all regardless of the goal. We cannot let hitting that terror barrier, or our fear of failure, stop us from achieving our dreams.

How do you build that great big dream? How do you turn that dream into a theory? How do you turn the theory into a goal? You say: "I'm able to do it" and "I'm willing". That's when you start to get emotionally involved, and if you genuinely endeavour to give it everything you have, you can go right through that terror barrier.

Understand what is causing the fear, because it is that understanding that enables you to go through it. Understanding is really the key to ***Freedom***. It does not eliminate fear or the chaotic vibration, but it allows you to overcome the emotion of fear.

Even when you have stepped through that terror barrier, and you are in the area of freedom, you will still experience fear. But the repetition of getting emotionally involved in the Y-idea means that eventually the X-conditioning disappears. That is when you have changed your paradigm and advanced to living in freedom. Once the Y-idea becomes bondage, it is time to move to the Z-idea - but you go on with experience, knowing that you have done it before.

You cannot eliminate the fear. Every time I set a new goal, it scares me. There are parts of my mind that tell me not to bother with the next challenge - to take it easy instead. We all have these thoughts and to succeed we have to kick those thoughts away. If what you are doing is not constituting growth, if it is not scaring you, then you are going in the wrong direction.

The beautiful truth is that whatever scares you, excites you at the same time. It excites you because on a conscious level this is what you want, and it scares you because on a subconscious level you have never done it before. You are moving into a foreign vibration.

When you begin working towards a new goal, you will be looking outside of yourself for the resources you need to get you there. But you will not find them easily; they will not be immediately evident. You need to have faith, understanding and knowledge that everything you need is going to come as you need it. Remember, there is only one problem in the entire world and that is ignorance.

Everywhere you go, all problems have ignorance as their foundation – simply not knowing. The opposite of ignorance is knowledge. Understand that all the knowledge there ever was or ever will be is 100 percent evenly present in all places at the same time. The answers to our questions are already here.

Imagine an individual that has set their objective and is looking outside of themselves, but they do not see what they need to get to their goal. What is going to happen? They see worry come onto the screen of their consciousness, and they start to entertain doubt and internalise negative concepts.

They hit fear, and fear is a destructive emotion. They encounter anxiety and instead of expressing it, they suppress it. The suppression turns into depression, and the depression turns into *dis-ease*. Always hyphenate that word, do not just say disease, it is *'dis-ease'* – a body that is not at ease. And the dis-ease turns to disintegration.

There is a basic law of life that says: "Create or disintegrate." If you are not going ahead, you are going backwards. So, the challenge is to get away from the negative flow from doubt to worry, anxiety, suppression and depression.

Depression is anger turned inwards, so we have to move over to the positive polarity. Understanding comes from knowledge and we want to understand the laws of our being. We want to understand that even though we cannot see it, what we need is coming. If we stay in the right vibration, we will attract it. But there is only one way of developing understanding and that is through study, which is the one thing that most people do not want to do.

There are many forms of study, but if you want to win, you have got to study. We want to understand that everything we require is going to be delivered to us exactly at the right time, so we start to build a positive picture of the good that we desire in our mind, and then we get emotionally involved with that positive picture. That sets up a vibration called *faith*.

Faith is the ability to see the invisible, to believe in the incredible, which permits us to receive what might appear impossible. Faith is the opposite of fear and understanding brings faith. Faith based on understanding can move mountains.

Faith also can be defined as an adhesion to what another affirms. This may be reasonable if there are adequate reasons, conversely this may be unreasonable if there are no adequate reasons. Human development is based on cognitive methods of understanding faith. Blind faith is ineffective, faith based on understanding the law of nature is the proven methodology for the creation of success.

Our life is made up of relationships; at the end of that life of relationships, history is established. History articulates the past, but simultaneously it influences the present and if we are in the outside-in education, we can shape the future with inside-out thinking.

By working with understanding we can develop a positive picture. We can see the good that we desire before it arrives, and we can get emotionally involved with it.

Faith expresses itself on a physical level, not as anxiety - but as well-being. Well-being is something we like to express, and that expression turns to acceleration. It picks up speed and attracts more good things.

Faith allows us to be calm. James Allen, the Harvard professor, once said: “Calmness of mind is one of the beautiful jewels of wisdom. It is the result of long and patient effort in self-control.” Being at ease allows us to create.

Make certain that what you are making happen is big and beautiful.

Do not mess around with little goals. Remember; *ignorance/knowledge*. We are all ignorant about certain things. I am ignorant about how to make a roast dinner or fix my car. I plan to stay that way. But there are some things that we should never be ignorant about, and that is how our marvellous minds work. You can do anything with your mind if you develop it. Build understanding and you will live in freedom, which is really the only way to be. If I want to be free, I have to be *me*: Not the me that I think you think I should be; not the me I think my parents think I should be. I have to be *me* if I am to be free and able to create.

I trust you are now starting to allow your thoughts to shift; to invite the change you would like to see. I hope that you are inspired and emotionally involved with the big goals that are worthy of your time.

When you act towards your goals, you might just run straight into the terror barrier. I know I do, all the time. If what you are doing is not constituting growth and is not scaring you, remember you are probably going in the wrong direction.

Embrace the terror barrier. Get excited about it, because it spells growth. Apply what you have learned from this chapter and learn how to move forward through the terror barrier, to achieve everything that is possible on the other side.

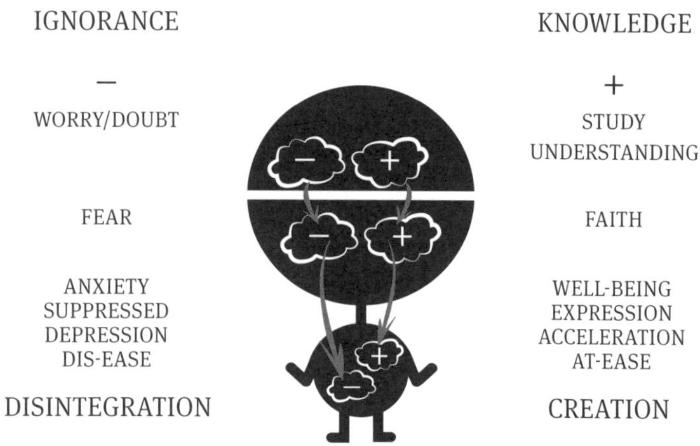

"Faith and fear both demand that you believe in something you cannot see. It's your choice" Bob Proctor

CHAPTER 8

YOUR BELIEFS WITH BEHAVIOUR

I hope that you have enjoyed studying and applying all that you have learned so far. Remember that constant spaced repetition is the key to success. Only by reading and re-reading these chapters will you grow in awareness of who you are and just how much you are uniquely capable of.

This chapter is about the value of belief. Belief, according to the Oxford English Dictionary is: "An acceptance that something/someone exists or is true, especially without proof." In this chapter we focus on belief in oneself. It is a basic human behaviour to reach out to *do* more and *be* more. If you want more from life and you want better results, then you must believe it is possible.

If you have limited self-belief, you will never go beyond where you think you can go. So, open your mind, because it is belief on a deeply subconscious level that controls your behaviour.

Frank Lloyd Wright, the American architect and educator, once said: "The thing always happens that you really believe in and the belief in a thing makes it happen."

We have heard that all things are possible for the person who believes. When Napoleon Hill wrote about this, he said: "There is a difference between wishing for a thing and being ready to receive it." He argued that no one is ready for something until they believe they can acquire it. The state of mind must be belief and not mere hope or wish. He also said: "Open-mindedness is essential to belief. Closed minds will not inspire faith, courage or belief."

Hill added: "Remember, no more effort is required in order to aim high in life, to demand abundance and prosperity, than is required to accept misery and poverty."

Consider his idea about the difference between wishing for something and being ready to receive it. The state of mind must be belief and not a mere hope or wish. I find this a pretty interesting concept.

Prior to encountering the concept of inside-out education, I had a limited belief in myself. But in a relatively short period of time, my business grew from nothing into a multi-million-pound business spanning the UK, Canada, USA, Dubai and India.

That was achieved because my belief system changed. Our belief system is based on our evaluation of something; if we re-evaluate that situation, our belief about it will frequently change. You will never go beyond where you believe you can go. But the more you study *you*, the more you understand you, and the more you are going to believe that your goals are achievable.

Think of this for a moment: the electrical system in your body would make the electrical system in a super-computer look like a toy. Your blood circulates through hundreds of miles of passageways and every 33 seconds it carries all the, sugars, oxygen and hormones in and all the waste out in one sweeping change.

Your brain is an electronic switching station, with every cell having both a negative and a positive pole, based on the law of polarity. You activate brain cells and set up a vibration in your body, and if you activate the negative pole in any cell, you are going to move yourself into a negative vibration. By just switching over to the positive pole, you move into a positive vibration.

Stop and ask yourself what happens if you cut your hand. It heals, thanks to the healing power within you. You have an ingenious system within you to keep your body in working order.

But still you find people who do not believe in themselves. I did not believe in myself because I did not understand myself. I understood very little: I thought I was my name and this body. But you are not your body, and your name is something you were given. You can change it.

Praxis is the integration of belief with behaviour, and that makes praxis an extremely powerful word.

According to my mentor Bob Proctor, we have belief on two levels. We have a belief in our educated mind based on logic, what we see and the information we gather. But we also have a belief on a much deeper, subconscious level, which controls our behaviour. That is part of the paradigm. Most of your beliefs did not originate from you but were passed along in your genes as part of your conditioning and by the environment in which you are living.

To make something happen, we have got to understand this word, praxis. We have got to begin to integrate some of our beliefs into our behaviour. It is not enough to believe we can do better. We must make that happen.

We come back to the Knowing-Doing gap. You need to really believe what you are capable of. The beautiful truth is that no one knows what you are capable of. The most learned scientists alive will not even guess at what you and I are capable of.

We have more power in our little fingers than would be required to light an entire building for nearly a week. Apparently, there are several million-kilowatt hours per pound of potential energy locked up in the electrons in the atoms of our bodies. We are walking masses of power. When people say they do not have the energy, they mean they do not have the desire.

Remember, Hill said: "There's a difference between wishing for something and being ready to receive it. No one is ready for a thing until they believe that they can acquire it. The state of mind must be belief and not mere hope or wish." He also said: "Open-mindedness is essential to belief."

He pointed out that a closed mind will not accept an idea that it is not familiar with. When your mind is closed and an idea comes along, you reject it. Instead, you need to open your mind.

This is down to the laws of the universe. You might have seen *The Secret* by rocket scientist Dr Wernher von Braun, which asserts: "The natural laws of this universe are so precise that we don't have any difficulty building spaceships. We can literally send people to the moon and we can time the landing with the precision of a fraction of a second."

These natural laws are very important, and we want to understand them. Our minds operate according to laws. The thoughts that we internalise set up a vibration. The vibration causes an action. The action causes a reaction. The action-reaction creates the result.

As I interpret them, the Natural Laws of the Universe are:

The **Law of Perpetual Transmutation** says that energy moves into physical form and the images that you hold in your mind most often will materialise in results in your life.

The **Law of Relativity** [a separate concept from Albert Einstein's theories of Special and General Relativity] says nothing is good or bad, big or small, until you relate it to something, and that relating your situation to something worse will mean yours will always look good.

The **Law of Vibration** states that everything vibrates, nothing rests. The conscious awareness of vibration is called feeling. Your thoughts control your paradigms and your vibration, and when you are not feeling good, it is useful to become aware of what you are thinking, then think of something pleasant.

The **Law of Polarity** says that everything has an opposite: Hot—Cold, Up— Down, Good—Bad. Constantly look for the good in people and situations and, when you find it, tell people. People love compliments and the positive idea in your mind makes you feel good. Remember, good idea—good vibration.

The **Law of Rhythm** means the tide goes out, night follows day and good times follow bad. When you are on a downward swing, do not feel bad. Know the swing will change and things will get better. There are good times coming— think of them.

The **Law of Cause and Effect** means that whatever you send into the universe comes back. Action and reaction are equal and opposite. Say good things to everyone, treat everyone with total respect and it will all come back. Never worry about what you are going to get, just concentrate on what you can give.

The **Law of Gender** states that every seed has a gestation or incubation period. Ideas are spiritual seeds and will move into form or physical results. Your goals will manifest when the time is right. Know they will.

Hill said: "Remember, it takes no more effort in order to aim high in life, to demand abundance and prosperity than is required to accept misery and poverty." Let us make certain that when we set our goals, we set them high. Internalise those goals until we believe in them on a subconscious level.

Praxis and belief are two very important words. Believe and succeed. All things are possible if you believe. What did William James, the American philosopher, say? "Believe, and your belief will create the fact." Praxis is the integration of belief with behaviour. Put it to work.

Beliefs shape your results. If you think you will fail your exams, you will not become motivated to prepare and later, when you take the exams, you will fail. That's how beliefs can shape reality.

It is the same when you are looking for a job. If you think you will never find a good job, you will not be motivated to prepare properly and so, when you try to find a good job, you will fail.

Think about your driving test, when you truthfully believed you could pass, you did; when you had doubts, you failed. Please try and go back to a memory and do a self-appraisal of your winning and losing. You will then understand this concept.

By simply changing your beliefs, you can achieve anything!

If you believe you are capable of an A in your exams, then you will be motivated to study hard and prepare so, when you take the exams, you will almost certainly get an A.

Napoleon Hill said: "No one's ready for a thing until they believe that they can acquire it. The state of mind must be belief, not mere hope or wish." That is what praxis is all about – integrating belief with behaviour. You can do anything, but you must believe it. If you don't believe it, it is going to be a struggle.

Look at Walt Disney. Today, the Disney brand earns billions of dollars from merchandise, films and theme parks around the world, but Walt Disney himself had a difficult start. He was fired by a newspaper editor because he apparently "lacked imagination and had no good ideas".

After that, he started several businesses that ended in bankruptcy and failure. However, he had a deep-rooted belief in himself and his ideas. He combined this belief with his behaviour, by not giving up. Eventually, he found a recipe for success that worked. This is part of the proven methodology of the creation of success.

The content of this chapter has had a massive impact on me on a personal level. I had to look really hard to see what my self-limiting beliefs were, because they were buried deep in my subconscious mind, which is my paradigm. I encourage you to do the same. Think hard about what is holding you back, and then believe you can change it.

CHAPTER 9

THE MAGIC WORD

Now it is time to think about attitude, and what attitude means to you. What kind of attitude did you bring into reading this chapter? Is it enthusiastic and open-minded or closed and a bit negative? Are you even aware of your own attitude, because many people are not? Most people have an awareness of their thirst, hunger, happiness and stress but not of their attitude.

In this chapter we are going to explore the key role played by attitude in the creation of success. You can choose which direction to take your mind – positive or negative. It is your choice. I really love this concept and it has made a big difference in my own life.

I believe your attitude rubs off on your peers, your tutors, your family, your friends and all those who come into contact with you. A positive attitude is infectious and spreads positive energy.

But attitude alone will not, of course, get you the results you want –

you also need ability, talent and the requisite skill and knowledge. But without a good attitude, your skill and talent will not get you very far, and many people fail to realise that. The key to success is attitude - not just knowledge or talent.

Two common types of poor attitude can cause big problems in life.

First, an attitude of "It is not my fault and I really don't care anyway".

There is a huge culture of excuses in society in general. There is a lack of accountability for poor grades or bad behaviour. "It is not my fault" means no one takes responsibility.

Students blame their tutors, parents or circumstances for their poor marks but really, they just did not study hard enough, perhaps because of their paradigms. Workers blame train delays for constantly being late to the office, but if they had changed their paradigm of being disorganised and woken up earlier, they would not only have made it on time but also had more time to prepare for the day.

Similarly, there is an attitude of "I want a rich and easy life".

Many of the celebrities we see in today's magazines and on TV are famous for very little reason, other than being famous. They are photographed in expensive designer clothes and on holiday in exotic locations; materialism is rife and there is a lack of aspiration.

Dating a famous footballer is an easy means to free money. Reality TV offers instant fame. So why bother working hard at school, college, university or in work? That kind of attitude will not bring you success or happiness.

Education is absolutely sacred. At Regent Group, our ethos is "The end of education is character"; and I believe that there is always room for continual character development. The key to success lies entirely in our own attitude. So, let us learn about attitudes.

Think back to the stick person concept; I don't think you can go over it too often.

The stick person is really the genie and the more you get to know this, the more you understand it – the more you are going to realise what an absolute genie it really is.

Now remember the top circle is the mind, and the bottom one is the body. The body is the instrument of the mind. It does exactly what the mind tells it to do.

If you look at your body in a very simple manner, it is a molecular structure and a mass of energy. It is in a very high speed of vibration. Your mind activates your brain cells and determines what vibration you are in. Attitude is everything. William James, the American philosopher and psychologist, said the greatest discovery of his generation was that human beings could alter their lives by altering their attitudes of mind.

The conscious mind – also referred to as the thinking mind or the educated mind – is where our intellectual factors are resident and our sensory factors are hooked up, allowing us to hear, see, smell, taste and touch. These are the motorways that hook us up to the outside world, and they can be a blessing and a curse. We look at what is going on around us and we want to control it. To do that we need to understand how the mind functions.

The conscious mind can gather information from outside and has the ability to originate information. There is a power flowing to and through you that I refer to as a pure unadulterated life force. A scientist would call it energy. As it flows into your consciousness, it is either negative or positive. The positive and the negative represent the law of polarity, which says that everything has an opposite. There is a positive and a negative pull and you need both. When power flows into us, we make it what it is. We have the power to make it negative or positive by virtue of our own thoughts.

Your educated mind can think, to accept or reject. So, as ideas and information come into our consciousness, we can determine whether we want to accept them and let them be a part of our life.

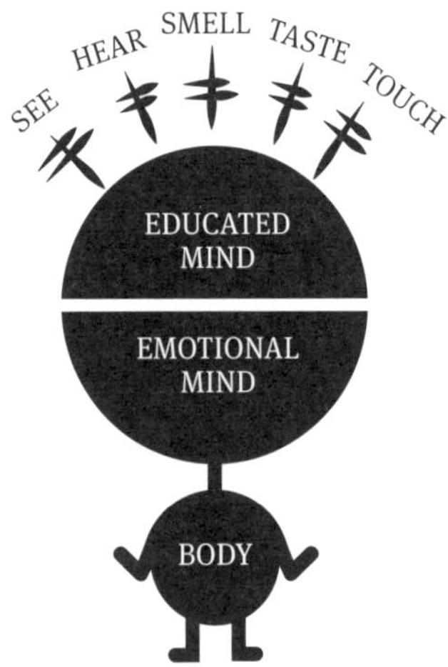

You can choose your thoughts with your conscious mind and thoughts cause your feelings in your emotional mind. Your emotional mind then causes the vibration or, in other words, the action.

Imagine you know you have a poor attitude in your morning meeting. Your attendance is terrible and when you do show up, you are late. Your preparation work is not completed on time and you do not put much effort into participating. Your thoughts and attitude are not positive. Mornings have never been your best point of the day – you were told this years ago by a teacher and it went straight into your sub-conscious mind. Your current boss is not impressed by your lack of effort to start the day positively, which is evident in their attitude to you. Because the boss acts frustrated with you and is more positive with your peers who are trying, this exacerbates your bad attitude towards the meeting.

But what if you want to change your bad attitude? You need to change the thoughts that come into your conscious mind. When you start to think negatively of the meeting, the boss or the colleagues in the meeting, the only answer is to change those thoughts to positive and turn it around.

Every time a negative thought enters your mind, tell yourself that the meeting is going to help you get on in your career, and that your boss does care about you and would have more positive interactions with you if you made the effort too. Tell yourself that you can make a really valuable contribution if you turn up on time and do some preparation. Tell yourself this every day, every time a negative thought enters your mind. This will filter down to your subconscious mind and will cause an emotional response.

You will find that with enough repetition, you will start changing your behaviour and will ensure you attend meetings on time, that your preparation is completed and that you speak up and make a positive impression. You will make the effort to bring a great attitude to every meeting and to smile at your peers and engage in the discussion. Suddenly, your whole world will change.

Your new attitude will bring a very powerful change of results. Your work will improve, your relationship with your boss and your peers will improve. You will have a great attitude and going to your meetings will become a positive experience and a great start to the day.

The same applies to things we hear externally. We frequently watch the news or listen to the radio and hear that the economy is going to be bad. If you do not want it to be a bad, just reject that idea. You see even in the very worst economy, there are people experiencing a great economy.

During the Great Depression of the 1930s, there were people earning millions of dollars. Not everyone succumbed to what was going on outside. When someone shares something with you that is negative, it could be real and it could be accurate, but get rid of it. Do not entertain or internalise it. Remember that you can accept or reject.

I learned this concept from Bob Proctor and I have been using it ever since.

When someone comes up to me with something negative that is not doing anybody any good, I just say "that's interesting", and then I change the subject. I do not get caught up in it. Instead, I talk about the person I am talking to and what they do well, causing the subject to switch in a heartbeat. Try it – it is very powerful.

The conscious mind can originate ideas and accept or reject realities. But the subconscious mind does not have that ability and is totally deductive. In other words, it can only accept, not reject, and it accepts everything that comes to it as real.

Think about that for a moment. It has no ability to reject. Mentally relax and build a beautiful picture on the screen of your conscious mind. It could be from the past or it could be something you think is going to happen in the future. Just close your eyes and let yourself get emotionally involved and entice your imagination. Imagination is the most valuable tool with which humankind has been gifted.

Your subconscious mind will take it and accept it as if it is happening now. Because the truth is, in your mind, it is happening right now. In the mind, all you have is now, and your subconscious mind will accept whatever you give it as real.

If you get involved in we think of as *imagined reality*, it is a beautiful concept. You are turning your world into something that you want it to be.

Some people say that is not realistic, but it is what got us to the moon, built the internet for us, and got pioneer Edmund Hillary to the top of Mount Everest. It put the Wright brothers in the air and brought us 3D-printed organs.

So, if your peers or colleagues laugh, let them laugh, and say, "That's interesting". Realise your subconscious mind will accept what you give to it. In the 21st century, virtual reality and augmented reality technologies will further accelerate humankind's abilities to imagine. It will certainly boost their capacity.

Let us put the two parts of the mind together. Here we are on the conscious level with the ability to take this power that flows into our conscious mind and build whatever we want out of it.

We can accept ideas that come in from the outside world; reason with them and accept them. We can turn those images over to our subconscious mind and it will accept them as real. Whatever is impressed on the subconscious mind controls the vibration of the body. So, your mind-body is going to be in any vibration that is dictated by the ideas that you impress upon your subconscious mind. With a negative idea, you will move into a bad vibration. With a positive idea, you will instantly move into a positive vibration.

If you are mentally and physically in a bad vibration, that is all you can attract. When you take a positive idea and internalise it, you move into a positive vibration. You begin to attract positive energy and people who are in a positive vibration. This is how you literally control you.

Victor Frankl was a psychiatrist who spent the war years in a Nazi concentration camp, and in his best-selling book, *Man's Search for Meaning*, he described his experience.

He said: "We who lived in concentration camps can remember the men who walked through the huts comforting others, giving away their last piece of bread. They may have been few, but they offer sufficient proof that everything can be taken from a man but one thing: the last of the human freedoms – to choose one's attitude in any given set of circumstances, to choose one's own way."

Regardless of the emotional and physical abuse that man is subjected to, he was able to hold a positive idea on the screen of his mind. No one can cause you to think something you do not want to think – you have the freedom to think anything you want. That is where a person is truly born free. Thinking is the highest function of which you are capable, and it is those thoughts that control your feelings, and your feelings control your actions.

Your attitude will determine where you go in life. It is everything, including the foundation of either failure or success: bad attitude leads to bad results, and good attitude to good results.

Attitude is a difficult thing to define, but similar to character, attitude is the composite of our thoughts, our feelings and our actions: thoughts in the conscious mind; feelings in the subconscious mind; and actions in the body. It is much like a cake: the composite of several different ingredients all brought together. Your thoughts, feelings and actions are the energy that you send into the universe, and whatever you send out is going to come back to you. The actions we create have an equal and opposite reaction.

In fact, it comes back while you are sending it out. Nature abhors a vacuum, so if you concentrate on a positive idea, you activate positive polarity on cells in your brain, and you send off a positive charge of energy. As you send off that positive energy, you simultaneously take on an equal amount of like energy. As you send it out, you take it on, and you can set up a magnificent vibration.

I have students that come to me and tell me their place of study or teacher has a negative attitude. I look at them and say, “change it”. One person really can change the world, and that is you.

One person changed my world. I might be one person sharing this information that changes your world, just as you can change the world of the people you deal with, if you have the right attitude.

Attitude is a magnificent word, because it really is the key to everything you are ever going to achieve. Keep your attitude right. If somebody has a bad attitude, move away from them, because you probably cannot change their attitude. You can certainly help them, but you cannot do it for them. But you sure can do it for yourself. You want to become your own best friend, and attitude is the magic word. The stick person is the genie.

Attitude is literally the foundation of failure or success. Are you inspired to change the way you see the world? Your attitude governs the way you perceive the world and the way the world perceives you. You really can choose to perceive things differently from right now.

CHAPTER 10

THE MOST VALUABLE PERSON

Consider whether you are a leader or a follower. Do you know how to lead yourself? If not, you will probably struggle to lead others. I would like to be both a leader and a follower. I am developing myself and learning when to lead and when to follow, because before you can become a good leader, you must be an intelligent follower.

This is a powerful chapter because it moves everyone towards a leadership role. An exceptional leader brings out the best in people and helps them feel good about themselves, empowering others. Leadership has no age barrier or constraints. Leaders are people of all ages who take the initiative and go for it.

We used to believe that leadership was inborn or took countless years of study, achievements and degrees. If you spent years climbing the ladder you could finally hit the top step that had "leader" written on it in bright bold letters, but that is no longer the case. The economic cost of failing to recognise young people as leaders is huge. Not appreciating the impact younger people can have is leaving a huge void in innovation, invention, and productivity.

You can apply the leadership principles in this chapter to everything you do; to your studies, your performance on your sports team, to making your voice heard at local and national government, to your career or apprenticeship, to volunteering in your local community, and even to your own start-up business. There are no limits.

I want to share an idea with you that literally changed my life by changing how I see the world. It changed how I work and how I deal with other people, and it came from Napoleon Hill's book, first introduced to me by Bob Proctor.

Napoleon Hill said: "Broadly speaking, there are two types of people in the world. One is known as leaders and the other is known as followers."

Decide at the outset whether you intend to be a leader in your chosen calling or remain a follower. As Hill said: "The difference in compensation is vast."

I had a goal of growing my business. So, when I heard from Bob Proctor and subsequently read that about compensation, I got wired into what I was reading. He said: "The follower cannot reasonably expect the compensation to which a leader is entitled, although many followers make the mistake of expecting such pay." He said: "It's no disgrace to be a follower. On the other hand, it's no credit to remain a follower." He added: "Most great leaders began in the capacity of followers. They became great leaders because they were intelligent followers.

With few exceptions, the person who cannot follow a leader intelligently cannot become an efficient leader." There is much to learn about great leadership, not only by studying those amongst us, but by reading and studying great leaders of the past.

If you wish to become a leader, I highly recommend you find a trustworthy mentor or mentors who you really admire and ask them to be your personal coach. Ask them to share their valuable life lessons with you and guide you in your chosen goals. Mirror their good attitude and behaviour.

The word mentor comes from the character Mentor in Homer's epic tale, *The Odyssey*. Mentor was a trusted friend of Odysseus, the king of Ithaca. When Odysseus fought in the Trojan War, Mentor served as friend and counsel to Odysseus' son Telemachus.

Having a mentor will help shape you into a very effective leader. A leader is a person who inspires people to follow them because they want to. People want to follow the leader who has vision and knows where they are going, because people can buy into that vision. But first, you need to become an intelligent follower – the best follower that you can become.

Napoleon Hill's book, and the teachings of Clayton M. Christensen and Bob Proctor, led me to the work of Earl Nightingale. In his *Lead the Field* programme, Nightingale talks about leading. We can look at his work in the context of leading in today's new economy, which is not the same as the economy that we were born into. Nightingale said: "Every business, every organisation, from the smallest to the largest, needs a leader."

The attitudes of the people working in any organisation reflect the attitude of the leader, and that leader is always just one person.

Chris Haggerty, a management consultant, says: "The goal of most leaders is to get the people to think highly of them as a leader. But the goal of the exceptional leader is to get the people to think highly of themselves."

Nightingale told a story in his book about the Great Depression, when so many businesses had great signs hanging outside saying "No help wanted". Earl knew a man that could get a job anywhere he desired at a time when most people would take any job they could get. He would study a company, study what they did, and then send a message to the president of the business.

He would say: "I have been studying your company and your industry, and I have some ideas that I believe you will be interested in, which will substantially improve the bottom line on your financial statement and grow your company.

This man could get an appointment with any executive he chose, because he had what all the executives were looking for. And he got a job wherever he wanted.

All organisations are looking for leadership, and a leader always has a great attitude. A leader will see the good in other people and attempt to create a situation that brings it out. The leader is the person that other people want to follow, who operates on a creative plain. The leader is a person who understands who they are. In other words, we need to develop our own inner leadership and learn to lead ourselves before we can lead anybody else.

Leadership means understanding who you are and taking control of your own life. It means having a good attitude regardless of what is going on around you and knowing that you have the capacity to create anything you want in your world. See yourself as that person and always see the best in other people. There is far more room at the top than there ever will be at the bottom, and you will just naturally gravitate to the top.

These ideas on leadership are not complicated. They are simple ideas that anybody can incorporate into the self-image that they hold of themselves. Hill talks about unwavering courage, which is based on the knowledge of one's self and one's occupation. No follower wishes to be dominated by a leader who lacks self-confidence and courage. No intelligent follower will pursue a leader like that for long.

Nightingale says: "The opposite to courage is not cowardice, it's conformity. It's just going along with the masses, doing whatever the masses are saying." Hill talks about the essential element of self-control, because if you cannot control you, you cannot lead.

If we lack the confidence to lead, we cannot make decisions. Leaders need "definiteness of decision" – to know where they are going and to have clear sight of their goal. The plan can change, but the goal cannot. Plans may not be perfect and need amendments, but the goal should always be clear.

Nightingale talked about: “The habit of doing more than you are being paid for”, arguing that if you are not doing more than you are being paid for, you are never going to be paid for more than you are doing. Think about that.

Most people wait to get paid before they do things, which is like standing in front of an oven and saying: “Give me the heat, then I will put on the gas.” It will not work.

There are more basic laws of leadership. You must have a pleasant personality. You need sympathy and understanding. Understanding, in particular, is really key because it is the polar opposite of worry and doubt; and understanding can only be accomplished through study.

There are many forms of study, but if you want to lead, you must understand who you are, and you must understand the other person. You will never understand the other person if you do not understand yourself.

You must also understand how to lead and be willing to assume full responsibility. Responsibility is the key to freedom. Harry Truman, the 33rd US president, had a little sign on his desk that said: “The buck stops here.” He took full and complete responsibility for the position that the country was is in because he was the leader and if he was not prepared to take responsibility, the country was not going far.

Finally, leaders need to learn to cooperate. These are basics that you do not necessarily ever master, but you can continually improve your abilities.

At this point it is worth comparing leadership and management. Leadership is primarily a high-powered right brain activity. It is more of an art. You have to ask the ultimate question of life and have an understanding of the law of nature in dealing with personal leadership issues.

Once you have an understanding of personal leadership issues, you then have to manage yourself effectively to create a life congruent with the purpose.

Management is the breaking down, the planning, the analysis, the sequencing, the specific applications, the time-bound left-brain aspect of effective self-governance.

Steven Covey explains this concept as: "Manage from the left, and lead from the right."

Let us go back to where we started. You are never going to be an effective leader if you are not an intelligent follower, so do not be afraid to follow. Follow the effective leader and you will learn how to lead so that soon people will want to follow you.

Help people to think highly of themselves and really understand who they are, and you will never have a problem leading other people. Remember that attitude filters down from the top.

Keep yourself in tune with the higher side of your personality and the energy that you send off is going to be the energy that comes back to you.

The goal of the exceptional leader is to get people to think highly of themselves. Understanding your role, both as a leader and a follower, is vital to your happiness and growth. Do not be afraid to follow. Follow an effective leader and you will learn how to lead whether that person is alive or no longer with us; their principles and methodologies remain true and pertinent.

You can apply these leadership principles to everything and there are absolutely no limits to when and where you can lead yourself. Learn as much as you can about yourself and you will be an effective leader. Discuss this concept of leadership with your peers and you may be surprised at your leadership potential. Next, you need to think about the kind of leader you want to be.

"As a leader of people, you have to be a great listener, a great motivator, be very good at praising and bringing out the best in people."

"Leaders should be visible, accessible and approachable, and never stop learning."

Richard Branson

CHAPTER 11

THE IMPRESSION OF INCREASE

Now that you have learned some great tools, which when applied, will bring you amazing success, we are going to look at your ability to create an 'increase'. A decrease comes when you compete with others, but if you leave each person you meet with the impression of increase – a feeling of benefiting from their interaction with you – that will not only make that person feel better but will also enrich your life.

Think about how you feel when your boss praises you for something you worked hard on, or when a friend notices you have lost weight, are looking well, or had a good haircut. You are left with a feeling of positive energy, and that is the same for others when you praise their achievements. You uplift them in a positive way.

What I cover in this chapter is probably what has made the biggest impact on my life – in my businesses, my friendships, literally everything, including writing this book. I am constantly thinking about how I can leave a person feeling like they have got more from interacting with me and now have a richer, more fulfilling life and career in their mind.

I recommend a book called *The Science of Getting Rich,* by Wallace D Wattles. Wattles was a famous American author whose writing is widely quoted and referred to in countless self-improvement books. He shares a valuable insight that everyone should read and understand when he talks about leaving every person that you meet with the impression of increase. He says your thoughts and actions must convey to others the impression of increase. People are always seeking a better life, more money, more status, so do everything that you do in the firm conviction that you are giving more to everyone. In doing so, you make others feel rich.

Think about that: If you just happen to be stopping by the canteen or library, give the person that is there a compliment, but make sure it is sincere and deserved praise.

Everyone deserves a compliment, so start looking for what other people do well and bring it to their attention. Let them know that you notice it and give them an idea that inspires them. If you see the best in other people, you are going to feel good all the time. Your whole world is going to improve.

Make people feel good because you have come into contact with them. It is one of the greatest rules that I have ever learned.

The compensation you receive from developing this into your character is so rewarding and goes way beyond the scope of your imagination. If you want rich rewards, leave every person with the impression of increase. There is a science to getting rich and we are not just talking about money but being rich in all aspects of your life. You can achieve an abundant life by doing things in a certain way.

Picture two 17-year-old identical twins who are each given £100 to start a business. They have very similar genes, they grew up in the same house, they share their parents and have similar intellect, but one makes a big success of their business and the other does not. They are dedicating the same amount of time to their business but only one business is successful. You do not get rich as a result of genes and intellect. You become a real pro in your field by doing things in a certain way.

The more successful business-owner twin will be the one that has studied natural laws and read the information covered in this book and implemented these core principles into their business.

They set the goal of developing a profitable business within a specific period of opening, wrote that goal on a goal card, saved it to their phone and looked at it every day and every night. They understood their Knowing-Doing gap and changed their paradigm of being shy to one of an outgoing individual, who spoke with and engaged with prospective customers on a daily basis, thus building relationships and gaining more business.

Each of their customers was left with a feeling of increase. They also worked on their mental toolbox and strengthened their *Perception*, *Will*, *Imagination*, *Memory*, *Reason* and *Intuition* mental faculties. This enhanced not only their business skills, but also their ideas for growing the business. Their intuition told them to add another product line to the business, which increased profits significantly. Their goal was to create more and change the world. Think about how Steve Jobs changed our world.

The other twin put in the same amount of time but most of it was wasted. They were not exposed to the same teachings and did not focus upon their goal, so they lost their initial passion for the idea within a few days. They did not change their paradigm of shyness, so meetings with customers were awkward and did not result in new business. They did not work on their mental faculties and therefore did not believe their intuition on how to improve their business.

Instead, they spent time stressed and concerned about why the business was failing. They felt competitive and could not believe that their twin was doing so much better and, worse still, that their twin was not content with just doing well but was continually improving the business.

Think about Usain St Leo Bolt, widely considered the greatest sprinter of all time.

Despite recently retiring, he is still the best on the planet at what he does because he has smashed so many new world records. He achieved the world record of just 9.58 seconds in the 100m race and did not stop there. He continued to push himself to additional new world-record breakthroughs.

An eight-time Olympic gold medallist, Bolt won the 100m, 200m and 4 × 100m relay at three consecutive Olympic Games – a triple-treble that will be very difficult for anyone to replicate. He was not competing against anyone else; he was competing against himself.

The Science of Getting Rich, the science of being the best in your field, is not about doing certain things, but doing things in a certain way. There are laws that govern this whole universe and you must understand these laws. If you do not, the odds are pretty good that nothing of any consequence is going to happen, because it is going to happen on a hit-miss basis.

There are some people that, by some stroke of luck, just start doing things in a certain way and keep getting better and better and better. But they cannot tell you why. Luck is defined as the readiness to meet an opportunity.

I have learned some of the basics for really improving the quality of my life and that is what *Thinking into Character* is all about; the basics. One of the basics is that you do not become the best in your field by doing certain things, you become the best by doing things in a certain way.

You must be calm and confident and know who you are. James Allen, the Harvard professor, said: "Calmness of mind is one of the beautiful jewels of wisdom. It's the result of a long and patient effort in self-control." Self-control is one of the basic qualities of leadership. I am working on this, from a personal standpoint, but I fully acknowledge I have a long way to go…

Johann Wolfgang von Goethe, a German philosopher and writer who helped shape the thinking of the entire modern Western world, said: "Before you can do something, you first must be something."

You must do things in a certain way and bring your mind into harmony with the laws that govern your being. You need to understand that your thoughts control your emotions and your emotions control the vibration that your body is in and how you act.

If you do not spend time understanding the relationship between the conscious mind, the subconscious mind and the body, you are dealing with a hit-miss situation. Life is short. It can be a beautiful journey, but it can also be a headache if we do not understand how to make things happen. That is knowing about the creation of success.

The law says that what you put out comes back. We just want to put out the very best, regardless of what anyone else is doing. If you are going to win, you must be courageous.

American author and speaker Earl Nightingale said: "The opposite of courage is not cowardice, it's conformity. It is just going along with everybody else."

Don't do what everyone else is doing because you will end up where they are, and that is not excelling.

You want to stand out like a beacon on a dark night. You want to be the most effective person that you can be. The one point that all great leaders have agreed on is that you become what you think about, and not just those thoughts that you consciously entertain. We have all kinds of ridiculous, negative thoughts that come flying through our consciousness, but we become the thoughts that we take, internalise and get emotionally involved with. The thoughts that we let control us.

When you start your career, do not let the people around you control how you think about the company you work in. Think great thoughts about your company and understand that when you talk to somebody, you are the company. Great companies develop great people, and you can develop great people.

You do not become the best by doing certain things. You become the best by doing things in a certain way. Make *Thinking into Character* a part of your way of thinking. Make it a part of your way of life and you will have an amazing life. Make up your mind that regardless of what you did in the past, you are going to do something phenomenal in the future - right here, from today.

When you wake up in the morning, make up your mind that today you are going to do it better than you have ever done before. You are going to do it in a certain way. There is always a better way and what is best today is not necessarily going to be best tomorrow. But do the best every day.

Let us conclude this chapter with a law that operates all the time, with every person, everywhere. This is the Law of Compensation, which says the amount of money you earn is always going to be in exact relation to the need for what you do, your ability to do it and the difficulty there is in replacing you.

This is an important concept to understand.

There are just three steps – the need for what you do, your ability to do it, and the difficulty there is in replacing you: simply the demand, the skill and the supply. Ask yourself whether there is a need for what you do, and then focus on the second step by becoming better and better at what you do. Every day you are going to perfect it just a little bit more, and in so doing, you are going to become difficult to replace.

No one is indispensable.

There is a poem called *The Indispensable Person*, which says: "Put your hand in a bucket of water. Put it in up to the wrist, pull it out and the hole that remains is just how much you'll be missed. You can splash all you want as you enter, you can stir up the water galore, but take it out and, in no time, it'll be much the same as before."

There is no indispensable person but there are some that are very difficult to replace. I mentioned Usain Bolt earlier. His assets are worth more than £45 million, yet he earned only £1.7 million from winning races. He is paid millions of pounds just to show up at events or act as a global ambassador for major sports brands. He draws crowds like no other sprinter and is the very best at what he does.

Make up your mind to become very good at what you do. Give it everything you have and do things in a certain way. You are going to become very difficult to replace and, when that happens, your value will increase. If your employer does not recognise that, someone else will. The opportunities are always there for the person who masters what they do. You do not get rich by doing certain things, you get rich by doing things in a certain way.

This is a phenomenal concept that has guided my life after studying this material, and I have been richly rewarded. Everything

I do, I do in a certain way. I have found that, even after much self-study, I really do not know much about myself and I am excited to learn more, because as I do, the more my world unfolds.

We are like flowers that bloom. When we stare at a rose, it unfolds before our eyes, but we will never see a petal move. If you try to force the unfolding, we will kill it. A rose is one of the most beautiful expressions of life and you are, without question, one of the most magnificent expressions of life. If you do everything in a certain way, you will transform in just that way.

That feeling of increase feels good, and you are going to feel good all the time if you leave others with the impression of increase. If you see and highlight the best in people, you are going to be in a phenomenal place. You win and everyone wins. Steven Covey talks about this in his *7 Habits of Highly Effective People* as the "win-win" habit.

The Law of Attraction says that what you put out is what comes back. Put your best out, all the time, every time, regardless of what anybody else is doing. Make certain you are one of the most effective human beings you can be. Do things in a certain way, as described throughout this book.

Every chapter in this book will enable you to access an educational system which is a proven methodology for the creation of success. Go back and look at the tools you have acquired so far and get to know them really well, because you will become what you think about.

CHAPTER 12

IT IS EASY TO WIN

In this chapter, we build on what you have learned so far and focus on some practical steps to achieving the goals you have committed to.

Sometimes, despite our best intentions, we lose focus of our goals, often because we have forgotten what we have learned. This is one reason why repetition is so important. We need to go back to each and every chapter to truly learn, internalise and implement what we have studied.

We learned that to act on a new idea calls for breaking old habits. An old habit is part of a paradigm and does not want to let go. As we begin to act on a new idea, we may have trouble caused by the conflict created by two ideas that are total opposites.

The way to change paradigms is by constant spaced repetition: write out your new habit, read it over-and-over, record it and listen to it again-and-again until your new habit takes over, but you also need to integrate with emotion and the law of nature.

The moment we lose sight of the goal, the old habit gains control. It is worth repeating this because repetition is one of the first laws of learning. Earl Nightingale explains this idea which would change our life – "to live successfully, one day at a time".

In order to win, we must learn how to make decisions. There is a corollary element that must go hand-in-hand with decision making, and that is commitment. We must make a committed decision with responsibility. Responsibility means our ability to be responsive.

The word 'decision' comes from Latin roots – *decidere* meaning 'to cut off', which is itself derived from *de* meaning 'from' and *caedere* meaning 'to cut'. Therefore, a committed decision means cutting from any other possibility. A true decision means you are committed to achieving a result, which is the effect and cutting yourself off from any other possibilities, which are the *habits* or the paradigms, which are the cause.

After making a true, committed decision, with moral responsibility - especially the difficult/challenging ones, we usually feel a tremendous burden is lifted from our shoulders.

A lifetime is comprised of days, strung together into weeks, months and years. Break it down into single days and tasks to be completed each day. A successful life is nothing more than repeated successful days coming together. Nightingale said that no one manages time, but we can manage activities.

Think of a single day as a building block with which you are building the tower of your life. Just as a builder can only place one stone at a time, you can only live one day at a time. It is the way in which the stones are placed that determines the strength of a tower. Take one task at a time, from the moment you wake up in the morning, until you go to sleep at night and keep your goal in mind.

Each day consists of a series of acts and the success of a day depends on the successful completion of those acts. If everything we do during a day is a success – done to the best of our ability – then we can fall asleep in the knowledge that we have done our best. That is the way to live.

Do each day all that can be done that day. You do not need to overwork or rush blindly into your work, trying to do the greatest possible number of things in the shortest amount of time. Do not try to do tomorrow's—or next week's—work today. It is not about the number of things you do, but the efficiency of each separate action.

Gradually, you will find yourself increasing the number of acts and performing them all much more efficiently. To get the habit of success, you need only to succeed in the small acts of each day. These create successful days, weeks, months, years, and lives.

Success is not a matter of luck – it can be predicted and guaranteed, and anyone can achieve it by following this plan. Almost before you realise it, you will have achieved your goal. Looking back, you will realise that your success was not attributable to any one day, week, or month, but to the consistent, unrelenting, successful succession of single days. This is the way a building is successfully built, one brick at a time.

Do not get impatient and let daily distractions throw you off course. Shake them off and stay on track: concentrate on each act of the day, from morning to night, and do each one successfully. Know that if each of your acts is performed successfully, or at least the majority, your life will be successful.

It is not what you know but what you get done that the world rewards and remembers. More people are held back from success because they do not know how to get things done than for any other single reason. The biggest barrier to a person's success is not a lack of brains or willingness but an inability to get things done.

Many people know what to do and almost do it on time. They *almost* get a top grade. They *almost* get the university or job they want. The 'almosts' are not lazy – often they are busier than the very effective few. But they wander around unfocused all day long and fail to accomplish much. They are held back by indecision, by lack of organisation, and by an over-attention to minor details.

It is the creators that raise the world's standard of living. It is the creators that win the big share of the world's rewards. The producers get things done and will not permit the almosts to knock them off course.

But how do we separate the important acts from the unimportant?

Consider this story of a single idea for which a man was paid $25,000, according to Earl Nightingale. The president of Bethlehem Steel Corporation met with an efficiency expert named Ivy Lee. The president told Lee that what was needed was not more knowing, but a lot more doing. He said that if Lee could show him a better way of getting things done, he would pay him anything he asked.

Lee said that he could give the President something that would increase his efficiency by at least 50 percent. He handed the man a blank sheet of paper and told him to write down the six most important things he had to do tomorrow.

The man did as requested. Lee then told him to put those six things in order of priority for the company. He told him to put the paper in his pocket, look at it first thing tomorrow, and start working on number one. He told him to stay with number one until it was completed. Then take number two the same way, then number three and so on until he must quit for the day.

He said not to worry if he only finished one or two, because he was working on the most important ones and the others could wait. If you cannot finish them all by this method, he said, you could not have finished them by any other method. Lee told the man to continue in this way for two weeks, and then send him a cheque for the value he thought appropriate.

The entire meeting took no more than 30 minutes. In a few weeks, Ivy Lee received a cheque for $25,000 – around half a million US dollars in today's money – with a letter saying the lesson was the most profitable he had learned in his life.

This idea was also largely responsible for turning what was then a little known company into one of the biggest independent steel producers in the world.

Think about taking things one at a time, in their proper order. Of staying with one act until it is successfully completed before going on to the next, one day at a time.

Try the $25,000 idea in your life. Write on a slip of paper or type on your mobile device the six most important things you must do. Then number them in the order of their importance. Then tomorrow morning, start to work on number one and stay with it until it is successfully completed, then move to number two, and so on. When you have finished all six, get another piece of paper or type on your mobile device and repeat the process.

You will be amazed at the order it brings to your life and at the speed with which you will be able to accomplish the things that need doing, in order of importance. This simple, but tremendously effective, method will take all the confusion out of your life and you will never find yourself running around in circles wondering what to do next.

Remember to live the best you can, one day at a time. You need not worry about tomorrow, or the next day, or what is going to happen at the end of the month. One day at a time, handled successfully, will carry you over every hurdle and solve every problem. You can relax in the happy knowledge that successful acts make successful days, which in turn build successful lives.

Doing a lot of unnecessary things successfully is a waste of time. Make certain that the acts you take the time to do efficiently are important acts that move you ahead, steadily, towards your goal.

It was the great Harvard teacher and psychologist William James who said, in effect, "let no student worry about the success of their efforts. If a student does the work before them each day as best they can, they will wake up one day to find themselves one of the most competent of their generation".

This plan works for everybody. It removes doubt, fear and worry and brings order into our lives. All any of us needs to do is face each day as it comes, knowing that we have only to succeed today to guarantee our future. In this way, we move steadily ahead, growing more competent and more confident with each passing day. Others may seem to shoot up faster and operate in fits and spurts, but it is to the steady that the rewards are eventually paid.

St. Edmund of Canterbury was right when he said: "Work as though you would live forever but live as though you would die today."

There is nothing mysterious about achieving outstanding success, it is completely within our individual control. It is simply a matter of doing certain things in a certain way, every day – that is all there is to it. There is no valid reason why you should not become successful in your education, your personal life and your career.

Remember, everything in the universe operates on the law of cause and effect. There are no exceptions, and nothing happens by accident – for every result, there is a cause. You only have to take care of the cause and the result will always, without exception, take care of itself. Good cause leads to good effect and bad cause leads to bad effect.

For the next 30-60 days, complete this exercise every night before going to bed, or first thing in the morning with a fresh mind. These are six simple tips for everyday planning as suggested by Earl Nightingale.

1. Carry a note pad for jotting down things to be done, or make notes on your iPad, laptop or mobile phone or other device.
2. Plan your day tightly. Schedule enough time to keep you moving.
3. Plan any meetings with your teachers, mentors, colleagues, customers or suppliers in a block, and use the time wisely.
4. Plan things you can work on or think about while you are in transit or waiting around. Have material to read or study available for odd moments that inevitably crop up.
5. The best way to stop wasting time is to schedule your time. Plan tomorrow tonight, and do not wait for tomorrow.
6. Everyone goes to bed at a different time each night, but as a rule, gets up at the same time every morning. Set your alarm an hour earlier and dedicate that time to personal study and research. Think how much more you could achieve by making an enthusiastic start every morning.

Many of the world's greatest entrepreneurs and leaders had excuses for not getting things done. But they have ignored the excuses and created their dreams. Remember Stephen Hawking said: "However difficult life may seem, there is always something you can do, and succeed at. It matters that you don't give up." He had plenty of reasons to give up but instead he became one of the most iconic physicists of our time.

Have a plan for tomorrow and start with intensity. A person who is doing their best today is truly alive, but a person who did their best yesterday is stagnant.

Work for results and live one day at a time, the best you can. It will have an almost unbelievable cumulative effect on your success. When we see a bricklayer starting on a building and putting the first brick in place, we can be struck by the size of the task ahead. But one day, almost before we realise it, they are finished. All the thousands of bricks are in place— each one vital to the finished structure and each one sharing its portion of the load.

By living one day at a time, one task at time, you achieve your goals and live the life you dream of. Remember to stick to your goals and you can make the world a better place.

The discipline you learn and the character you build from setting and achieving a worthy goal can be more valuable than the achievement of the goal itself.

Isn't that wonderful?

CHAPTER 13

POSITIVE MENTAL ATTITUDE

In this chapter, we return to the importance of positive mental attitude and expecting the best. Our attitude can be defined as, according to Earl Nightingale: "The position or bearing as indicating action, feeling, or mood."

It is our actions, feelings and moods that determine the actions, feelings or moods of others toward us, and which control, to a surprising extent, our success or failure.

It is then, our attitude towards life that will determine life's attitude toward us. We have seen how everything operates on the law of cause and effect. Everything we say or do will cause some effect. We are charged with producing causes, because the effect, or the rewards of our actions, will always take care of themselves.

That is why I say success can be guaranteed and will come to us every time if we live in a certain way.

Good attitude	**=**	**good results.**
Fair attitude	**=**	**fair results.**
Bad attitude	**=**	**bad results.**

Everything in life is controlled by the law of nature, which is the *modus operandi.* There are seven laws and I found it amazing how well Earl Nightingale included all of the laws in his book, *Lead the Field.* Studying all of them will heighten your level of understanding and give you greater control over your life. These natural laws are critical, and I have covered this in previous chapters.

No matter what a person does, whenever you find a person doing an outstanding job and getting outstanding results, you will find a person with a positive mental attitude. These people have the self-belief that they can accomplish what they set out to accomplish; that achievement is the natural order of things; and that there is no good reason on earth why they cannot be competent and successful. They have a healthy attitude toward themselves and, as a result, towards life and what they want to accomplish.

Because of this attitude, they achieve some remarkable things and come to be called successful, outstanding, brilliant, lucky and so on. They are quite frequently no more brilliant or talented than the majority of the people who surround them, but they have the required positive mental attitude. They find their accomplishments not too difficult simply because so few others are really trying, and so few others really believe in themselves.

Successful people come in all sizes, shapes and colours, and in widely varying degrees of intelligence, background and education.

But they have one thing in common, they expect more good out of life than bad; they expect to succeed more often than they fail; and as a result, they do.

Our environment, the world we create around ourselves, is really a mirror of our positive mental attitude. If we do not like our environment, we can change it by changing our attitude. The world plays no favourites; it is impersonal. It does not care who succeeds and who fails, nor does it care whether we change or not. Our positive mental attitude towards life does not affect the world and the people in it nearly as much as it affects us.

Not long ago, I read a line that said: "Life is dull only to dull people!" This is true. It could also have read: "Life is interesting only to interesting people." Or: "Life is successful only to successful people."

From a mental attitude standpoint, you must first become the person you wish to be.

A famous restaurateur was once asked by a newspaper reporter: "When did you become successful?" He replied: "I was successful when I was sleeping on park benches. I knew what I wanted to do, and I knew that I'd do it."

You see, his attitude had been one of success, of expecting success, long before the tangible rewards of success were earned.

I recently had lunch with the Vice-Chancellor of a well-respected UK university. He told me that when he took the role many years beforehand, he had made it his ambition to get the university into the league table's top ten.

He did indeed manage to do so, but he had completely forgotten about identifying that goal until he came across some related paperwork while working in his office. This demonstrates just how inbuilt in his subconscious that target become!

In a previous chapter we told you that the great German philosopher Johann Wolfgang von Goethe put it this way: "Before you can do something, you must first be something."

The people with the best attitudes are the same people who operate with a high level of awareness. Science and theology are the only points of reference you can go to in search of information with respect to your true potential. Both of these areas clearly indicate that nothing is either created or destroyed, which would indicate that all the knowledge there ever was, or ever will be, is 100 percent evenly present in all places at the same time.

All the power there ever was, or ever will be, is
100 percent evenly present in all places at the same time.

In other words, the way to fly an aeroplane has always been there. The Wright brothers merely became aware of the principles governing powered flight. Thomas Edison merely developed a higher degree of awareness when he improved the incandescent light bulb with better vacuums and thinner filaments.

It was awareness that took us out of a cave and put us in a condominium.

Act toward others and the world at large in exactly the same manner that you want the world, and others, to act toward you. Treat the members of your family as the persons they really are: the most important people in your life.

Carry out into the world each morning the kind of attitude you would have if you were the most successful person on earth and notice how quickly it develops into a habit. Almost immediately, a change will be noticed. Irritations that used to frustrate and annoy disappear. When some less-informed person gives you a bad time, stay on track. When someone cuts in front of you with their car or acts in any other manner that shows their ignorance and lack of courtesy, do not permit yourself to drop to their level. Do not let their unhappiness make you unhappy.

It is vital to recognise that everything is controlled by law. Ralph Waldo Emerson, the American philosopher, said: "Let him learn a prudence of a higher strain. Let him learn that everything in nature, even dust and feathers, go by natural law and not by luck."

Each of us shapes our own life, and that shape is determined by our positive mental attitude. But it is not always easy, and for most of us, learning this new habit takes time. Once it is mastered, our daily lives will be transformed - as if we have walked out of a dark tunnel into the bright, clear light of day.

A person with a poor attitude towards learning is not going to learn very much until they change their attitude. But very few people change their attitudes, because they do not know how. William James was right when he observed that a change in attitude will change your life. But teachers tell that to students, doctors tell it to patients, sales managers tell salespeople and counsellors tell couples who are having trouble, and rarely does a transformation take place.

When you see someone with a negative mental attitude towards others, the chances are they also have a poor attitude toward themselves.

They are probably unhappy about something, because a happy person reflects their happiness in their attitude. A person with a poor attitude most of the time is unhappy and frustrated most of the time, making them a human magnet for unpleasant experiences. When those experiences come, they reinforce their poor attitude and bring more problems.

For the person with a good attitude, the same principle holds true in reverse. Expecting the best delivers the best.

Why would a person persist in a poor attitude? In truth, we are so familiar with ourselves that we tend to take ourselves for granted, minimise what we can accomplish, and believe others can reach heights that we cannot. We tend to overlook the fact that there is enormous undeveloped potential within each of us and a great reserve of talent and ability that we habitually fail to use.

There are millions of human beings living narrow, darkened, frustrated lives – living defensively – simply because they take a defensive, doubtful attitude towards themselves and towards life in general.

When you begin to develop a positive mental attitude, you will realise you have put yourself on the road to what you seek. You are well on your way to joining the top three percent of people. You have prepared the ground and planted the seed.

The higher you go in any worthwhile organisation, the better the positive mental attitude you will find. Positive mental attitude is not the result of success, but success is the result of a positive mental attitude.

As your mind can hold only one thought at a time, make sure your thoughts are constructive and positive. Look for the best in people and ideas and be constantly alert to new ideas that you can put to use. Do not waste time talking about problems or poor health, unless you are talking to your doctor. It probably will not help you and it cannot help others.

Radiate the positive mental attitude of well-being and confidence and the attitude of the person who knows where they are going. You will find good things happening to you right away. Start this habit now, practise it consistently, and you will do it for the rest of your life.

CHAPTER 14

GREENER PASTURES

No matter what your goal may be, it is possible that the road to it can be found in the very thing you are doing now. It was not until he was completely paralysed and forced to reach into the resources of his mind that a courageous farmer got the idea of producing exceptionally good meat products on his farm. From this idea, one of the country's largest meat-packing companies was born. His farm contained acres of diamonds too. He had just never seen them before.

A farmer once poked a tiny pumpkin into an empty jug. The pumpkin grew until it completely filled the jug and could grow no more. When the farmer broke the glass jug, he had a pumpkin exactly the size and shape of the jug.

If we are not careful, each of us can make a similar mistake by *poking ourselves into jugs* that limit our growth. But it is we who do the poking – not our job, our company, our territory, the economy or the times. *We* do it.

At this point it is useful for us to come back to paradigms. Unless your parents fall into that very small, select group of individuals who are acutely aware of what is going on and keep their mind tuned into a positive polarity, you were probably poked into a jug before you were born, as a result of genetic conditioning. And then, after you were born, this conditioning was reinforced environmentally.

We should avoid such self-restriction and realise there is virtually no limit to our growth and development on the land on which we now find ourselves, with our roots deep in the soil of a working philosophy of life, and our minds and bodies in a climate of freedom.

People who become outstanding in their work are those who see their work as an opportunity for growth and development and who prepare themselves for the opportunities that surround them.

Preparation is the key. This means becoming so good, so competent at what we are doing, that we actually force the opportunities we seek to come our way.

It takes creative imagination to know that diamonds do not look like diamonds in their rough state, nor does a pile of iron ore look like iron or steel. Great opportunities lurk, constantly, in every aspect of the work in which we find ourselves.

In order to begin prospecting your acres of diamonds, you must start to develop a faculty called intelligent objectivity, which is the ability to stand off and look at your job as a stranger might, who considers your pasture greener than his own.

Surveys indicate that the great majority of people look at their jobs as being as far as they can go, as the end of the line. Instead, we need to realise that expanding and dynamic industries needs and seek the uncommon person who is prepared to share in its growth and will richly reward people of vision and action.

Let me share the old story of an African farmer who heard tales about other settlers who had made millions by discovering diamond mines. These tales so excited the farmer that he could hardly wait to sell his farm and search for diamonds himself.

So, he sold his farm and spent the rest of his life wandering the vast African continent, searching unsuccessfully for the gleaming gems that commanded such high prices on the markets of the world. Finally, in a fit of despondency, broke and desperate, as I remember the story, he threw himself into a river and drowned.

Meanwhile, one day the man who had bought his farm found a large and unusual stone in a stream that cut through the property. The stone turned out to be a great diamond of enormous value, and he soon discovered that the farm was covered with them. That farm went on to become one of the world's richest diamond mines.

The first farmer had owned, literally, acres of diamonds, but had sold them for practically nothing in order to look for them elsewhere. If he had only taken the time to study and prepare himself—to learn what diamonds look like in their rough state and to thoroughly explore the land he owned, he would have found the millions he sought, right there on his own property.

The thing about this story, when I first heard it from Bob Proctor, that so profoundly affected me and subsequently millions of others, was the idea that each of us is, at this moment, standing in the middle of our own acres of diamonds. If we only have the wisdom and patience to intelligently and effectively explore the work in which we are now engaged, we will usually find the riches we seek, whether they are financial or intangible, or both.

Before we go running off to what we think are greener pastures, let us first make sure that our own pasture is not just as green or perhaps even greener. Otherwise, while we are looking at other pastures, other people are looking at ours. Someone has said: "If the other pasture looks greener, maybe it is because it's getting better care."

There is nothing more pitiful, to my mind, than the person who wastes their life running from one thing to another, forever looking for the pot of gold at the end of the rainbow, and never staying with one thing long enough to find it.

Ralph Waldo Emerson said: "What lies before you and what lies behind you are tiny matters compared to what lies within you."

The great painter Vincent Van Gogh once said: "I dream my painting and then I paint my dream."

There is another story on this theme. A man from a small town amassed a fortune starting with a single service station. In the beginning when things were tough, he would ask himself each morning, "What can I do to improve my service to customers?"

That man is now retired, and his son heads the large, complex enterprise that all started with a small service station and a daily question that virtually guarantees success in any undertaking: "What can I do to improve my service to my customers?"

Joel Barker, who discovered the concept of paradigms, said: "To be able to shape your future, you have to be ready and able to change your paradigm."

In order to become a professional in a world of amateurs, we need to study three important subjects: our company, and the industry in which it operates; our job, and the next upward step in our career; and our people, since successfully serving and getting along with people will determine our success or failure.

The greener pastures are often right where we make them.

Repetition of these concepts is very critical for the creation of success. Frequently, all you need in order to make an enormous improvement is simply a reminder of things you've known – but have forgotten.

All things are possible if the motivation is strong enough. Altering paradigms is a very personal thing and requires a reasonable amount of discipline and motivation along with understanding. The motivation comes from seeing ourselves in a much better position than where we are now.

Remember these words:
No man can become rich without enriching others. Anyone who adds to prosperity must prosper in turn.

CHAPTER 15

A WORTHY DESTINATION

It is very common to find individuals who are intellectually brilliant and yet accomplish little with their lives, because their day-to-day actions produce mediocre results. In situations like this, you must understand that it is not the intellect of the individual that is the cause of their behaviour; it is their paradigm that is in control. Until the paradigm is changed, the results will remain the same.

Virtually every person knows how to do better than they are presently doing in almost every aspect of their life. But there is an enormous difference between knowing how to do something and doing it. The knowing has to do with the conscious mind; the doing has to do with the sub-conscious mind. Unfortunately, our educational system has conditioned us to believe that the knowing is all-important. We are, in fact, rewarded and recognised with degrees and diplomas to hang on the wall for being able to repeat information we have gathered.

It is sometimes instructive to compare human beings to ships, as Scottish philosopher Thomas Carlyle used to do. It is estimated that about 95 percent of us can be compared to ships without rudders. Subject to every shift of wind and tide, they are helplessly adrift, and while they fondly hope that they will one day drift into a rich and successful port, we know that for every narrow harbour entrance, there are a thousand miles of rocky coastline. The chances of their drifting safely into port are slim.

But the small percentage who have taken the time and exercised the discipline to decide on a destination – and to chart a course – sail straight and far across the deep oceans of life, reaching one port after another, and accomplishing more in just a few years than the rest accomplish in a lifetime.

Every person should do the same thing. Unless you can say, in one concise sentence, what your goal is, then the chances are good that you have never clearly defined your goal.

When we talk of goals, let us be specific. What is it that you want? You, as a person? What is it you would like very much to have, or to be, or to do, even though you may feel it is – for one reason or another – somewhat beyond your reach at the present time?

Proceeding successfully through life should be a matter of progressively setting and achieving goals, one after another, each a little better and more interesting than the last. Just as a ship can sail to only one port at a time, set your first port of call. When you reach it, and reach it you will, you can set a new goal, and then another. By following this meaningful and common-sense approach to life, you will be successful and accomplish more in five years that the great majority of people do in a lifetime.

But first you must set your first goal. Most of the confusion and indecision suffered by the majority of people is caused by their half-heartedly wanting so many things that they cannot decide which to go after first. As a result, they run in circles and often accomplish little or nothing at all.

The best definition of success I have ever been able to find says: "Success is the progressive realisation of a worthy goal."

This means that any person regularly engaged in achieving something that they consider worthy of them is successful. At the same time, it also means that any person not so engaged must be defined as not successful - at least temporarily.

Any person with a dream in their mind who is pursuing a worthy goal is successful. The uninformed always seem to equate success with money, but while money often accompanies success, it has nothing to do with success necessarily unless it happens to be a part of the goal. It is left to each of us to decide for ourselves what our goal is.

With such a simple definition of success, you would think everyone would be successful. Everyone should be and everyone can be, but it is estimated that only a very small percentage of us are. Of all the people you pass on the street, perhaps only about three out of a hundred can tell you what they are working towards. The rest are just drifting along, hoping something good will happen, or at least that nothing too bad will. They are letting circumstances and economic winds blow them this way and that.

If you visit a ship and ask the captain his next port of call, he will answer you in one sentence. Even though the captain of a ship cannot see his destination for fully 99 percent of his journey, he knows what it is, where it is, and barring an unforeseen and highly unlikely catastrophe, he will reach it if he keeps doing certain things, in a certain way every day.

Every person should do the same thing. Unless you can say, in one concise sentence, what your goal is, then the chances are you have not clearly defined it.

Thornton T Munger, a pioneering research scientist in the field of forestry, once said: "There is no road to success but through a clear, strong purpose. Nothing can take its place. A purpose underlies character, culture, position, attainment of every sort."

Define your own worthy destination, and only then will you have a chance of reaching it.

One of the destinations creation of success enables us to achieve is wealth. What is financial wealth? We can refer to this as 'money' for simplicity's sake.

Money is the harvest of our production. Money is what we receive for our productions and service as persons, and which we can then use to obtain the production and service of others. We can quite often accurately gauge the extent of our productions and service by simply counting the amount of money we receive for it. I am not suggesting that piling up a lot of wealth is important. What we are saying is money as wealth is important because it is the only reward which is completely negotiable…and can be used by everyone. Look at it this way. A diamond is more valuable than a lump of coal yet that's exactly what a diamond was at one time. And just as a lump of coal can be transformed into one of the world's most valuable objects… a human being can vastly increase their own value to the world.

1% of our population earns approximately 96% of all the money that is being earned. You can go right through our education system and not learn how to create wealth. The earning of wealth is an exact science.

Earl Nightingale gives us the formula: "The amount of money we receive will always be in direct ratio to the demand for what we do. Our ability to do it and the difficulty of replacing us."

"The good life is expensive. There is another way that does not cost as much, but it isn't any good."

Spanish Distiller

There are two kinds of people where money is concerned; there are the majority who cut back on their wants to fit their incomes and there are those who make their income fit their wants. They are in the minority.

Now you must decide which best suits you…

Ben Franklin gave us the secret to wealth. He said that he road to wealth lies in augmenting our means or diminishing our wants. Either will do. But the quickest way to wealth is to do both at the same time.

A balanced life is when a person is living a life when they are spending their days doing what they love to do and at the same time, they earn the amount of money they need to provide the things they want, to live the way they choose.

Achieving wealth is a goal-oriented activity. All you need is an organised plan as Napoleon Hill says, and the road map and the courage to press on to your destination knowing in advance that there will be problems and setbacks, but knowing also that nothing on earth can stand in the way or an organised plan, backed by persistence and determination.

We must be opulent in our thoughts. Do not 'think money' as such, for it is only one means of opulence, but 'think opulence', that is, largely generously, liberally and you will find that the means of realising this thought will flow to you from all quarters, whether as money or as a hundred other things not to be reckoned in cash.

We must not make ourselves dependent on any particular form of wealth, or insist on its coming to us through some particular channel – that is at once to impose a limitation, and to shut out other forms of wealth and to close other channels.

Have faith in yourself, and the quiet, firm, inner knowledge that you can and will accomplish your goal and reach your worthy destination.

Know that the answer you seek will come to you in their own time, if you keep looking for them.

Above all realise that money cannot be sought directly. Money, like happiness, is an effect, it is the result of a cause is valuable service with purpose and moral principles. This is the basic law of nature.

Keep money in its proper place. It is a servant, nothing more. It is a tool with which we can live better, see more of the world, and give our youngsters the education they need and a good start in life.

You need only so much food to enjoy good health; likewise you need only so much money to live comfortably, securely and well. Too much emphasis on money reverses the whole picture – you then become the servant the money becomes the master.

As author George Horace Lorimer put it: "It's good to have money and the things money can buy, but it is good too, to check up once in a while, and make sure that you have not lost the things that money cannot buy."

Finally, we must understand that throughout the universe, life unilaterally consists of circulation, this means a continual flowing around, and this is universal law.

When this law is understood our attention should be directed rather to the 'giving' than the 'receiving'. We must look upon ourselves as 'centres of distribution' and the better we fulfil our function as such distribution centres, the greater will be the corresponding inflow. If we choke the outlet, the current must slacken, and a full and free flow can be obtained only be keeping it open.

The answer is that we must always start from the point where we are; and if your wealth at the moment is not abundant on the material plane, you need not trouble to start on that plane.

It is not money but the love of money that is the root of evil; and the spirit of opulence is precisely the attitude of mind which is furthest removed from the love of money for its own sake.

CHAPTER 16

THE FORMULA OF SUCCESS

We have been taught to know the truth and that the truth will set us free, but there is only one thing to be set free from and that is ignorance. After seriously studying the mind, human potential and the results that the vast majority of people get, it is apparent to me that the reason most people do not go to their mind for the help they need is because they really do not understand how it functions.

The marvellous mental tools that we are gifted at birth, for the most part lie dormant throughout life and as a result, there is very little life, merely existence.

In my recent years of researching this philosophy, I have spoken to numerous people and it is only on a rare occasion that I find an individual who understands what the faculties of the mind are or how to develop them.

Over 90% of our population is conditioned from birth to live through their senses. Earl Nightingale quoted the American writer Archibald MacLeish when he said: "The only thing about a man that is a man is his mind, everything else you can find in a pig or a horse."

Earl then said that this statement was uncomfortably true. He went on to say that the human mind is the only thing that separates us from the rest of the creatures on earth. In fact, it is the faculties of the mind that separate us. Animals operate by instinct. When you and I were created, instinct was removed and our intellectual faculties were put in its place. Unfortunately, we are not trained to use them and living through our senses leaves us in much the same position as our pets, since they too can also see, hear, smell, taste and touch.

In order to reflect just a moment on the human mind, consider what it has accomplished. As you do, realise that we are developing so rapidly that we have come further in the realms of progress in the past 50 years than in all the preceding 10,000 years of human civilisation.

We have reached, in the area of ideas and human advancement, a plateau so high it was undreamed of by even the most optimistic forecasters as recently as 10 years ago. But every new idea triggers additional ideas, so that now we are in an era of compounding advancement on every front, and in every area, that staggers the imagination.

From landing on the moon to the great bridges that span our bays and rivers, the harnessing of the power of the sun, in our atomic plants and ships, every man-made thing you see and touch spawned from the most powerful agency in the world, the human mind. Dr Harlow Shapley of Harvard has said that we are entering an entirely new age of man. He calls it the psychotic age: the age of the mind. And you own one! The artificial intelligence revolution is going to change the world and we need to be ready.

But consider this. The standard forty-hour week looks likely to get shorter. This means that the average working person has, at their disposal, an enormous amount of free time. In fact, if you total the hours in a year and subtract the sleeping hours (if a person sleeps eight hours every night), you find they have almost 6,000 waking hours of which they spend less than 2,000 on the job.

Now, this leaves a person with 4,000 hours a year neither working nor sleeping. These can be called discretionary hours, with which one can do pretty much do as one pleases – one's mind is free.

Now, so you can see the amazing results in your life, I want to recommend that you take just one hour a day, five days a week, and devote this hour to exercising your mind.

Each of us tends to underestimate his, or her, own abilities. We should realise that we have, deep within ourselves, a reservoir of great ability – even genius – that can be tapped if we just dig deep enough. It is the formula of success.

Successful people are not people without problems, but people who have learned to solve their problems. No one is without problems, because problems are a part of living. Think about the image of the electrocardiogram, or ECG, so often shown in TV and film and used by doctors to check a heart's rhythm and electrical activity. The sinus wave rises and falls, with the familiar accompanying beeps, when we are alive; when we are not, the line goes flat. Likewise, life will always have ups and downs, which is natural – if not, we would be living dead.

But consider how much time we waste worrying about the wrong problems.

It is estimated that most people spend 40 percent of their time worrying about things that never happen; 30 percent worrying about things that are over and past and cannot be changed by all the worry in the world; 12 percent worrying needlessly about their health; 10 percent worrying about petty ,miscellaneous concerns; and just 8 percent on real, legitimate worries.

In short, 92 percent of the average person's worries take up valuable time, cause painful stress and even mental anguish, but are unnecessary.

There are two kinds of real legitimate worries: the problems we can solve and the problems beyond our ability to solve. Most of our real problems fall into the first group: the ones we can solve, if we learn how.

There must be millions of people today who feel they are being barred from the life they want because they look on problems not as challenges to be met, but as wide chasms beyond their ability to bridge.

A little research proves that successful people have the same kinds of problems. One of the very real benefits of working with a psychologist or psychiatrist comes from learning that there are hundreds of thousands – perhaps millions – of other people with problems identical to our own. So, the whole thing boils down to a matter not of problems, common to us all, but of our ability to solve them.

Dr Kenneth McFarland, the American author, once wrote: "Two percent of people think, three percent think that they think, and 95 percent of the population would rather die than think."

I am inclined to agree with him. Thinking is hard work, which is why Henry Ford said that so few people engage in it. There is, however, tremendous compensation for the person that learns to think constructively.

The only thing in the world that can allow you to achieve your goals is your mind and its effective use. We all tend to underestimate our own abilities, but we have deep capabilities within ourselves, a reservoir of great ability – even genius – that can be tapped if we just dig deep enough. That is the miracle of the mind and indeed the formula for success.

Humans are composed of five various states of consciousness. These include instinct, a manifestation of the physical plane, intellect, a manifestation of the mental plane, inspiration, which concerns the soul, and intuition and revelation, both of which are spiritual. Yet, whilst they are in some way, quite different, they share the same core. A parallel can be drawn to milk which can be consumed in its simplest form, or in yoghurt, cheese or ice-cream. Many people align naturally to one of these planes over others.

As our bodies regenerate every second of the day, we attract atoms which reflect our intelligence which in turn reflects our thoughts. This can be said to be true of all people, from modern man to the tribesmen of old. As man grew more civilised, intellect began to play a greater part than instinct in everyday behaviour. What once would have been obvious, without considered thought, became less so.

Whilst death brings about the cessation of the physical and mental states, the other states of consciousness do not rely upon the existence of a body as their conduit.

Inspiration can be achieved in a myriad of ways, from reading, viewing art, or admiring the natural magnificence of our landscape. Yet, when we do not appreciate such things, it places limits on our capabilities and our possibilities.

Imagination is key and can be used by all states of consciousness. It is used to create everything both in ourselves, and the world around us. Sometimes, people confuse intuition and impression. This is understandable. Intuition comes from within but sometimes these intuitions are overridden by distrust from our own intellect. Intellect is a marvellous thing, the world today would not exist as it is without it, but it should not dominate, nor over-ride, our other faculties. Whereas impressions come from the objective world and should not be followed without careful thought as their origin is unknown.

CHAPTER 17

DESTINY IN THE BALANCE

We all seek rewards and understand that rewards come in two forms: tangible and intangible. That is, rewards include the money we earn, the home we buy, the car we drive and the clothes we wear. They also include the way we feel; our happiness, our peace of mind, our inner satisfaction and the people we meet and enjoy spending time with.

But remember, whatever it is you seek in the form of rewards, you must first earn in the form of service to others. All attempts to sidestep this law will end in failure, frustration and, if maintained long enough, ultimate demoralisation.

We see this frustration all around us, but a huge proportion of that frustration is due to a simple failure to understand this simple and wonderful law of nature. Consider whether you fully understand this law, both intellectually and emotionally. If you do, you will chart a wonderful course through life.

We introduced the concept of praxis in a previous chapter, which is the integration of belief with behaviour. We may find that a number of our beliefs have not been integrated with our behaviours. We say we believe something and on an intellectual level we do but, on an emotional level, we are programmed with information that is frequently the opposite.

It is quite common to grasp something intellectually and totally miss it on an emotional level. It is the emotional mind that is manifested in our physical results.

Earl Nightingale made the point that when we fully understand these great laws, both intellectually and emotionally, we can and will chart a wonderful course.

Consider the person sat in front of the empty fireplace saying: "Give me heat, and then I will give you some wood." People are divided into those who understand that the wood must be put in before they can expect warmth, and those who feel they should get warmth whether they do anything about it or not, or who feel they should get maximum heat from just a small supply of wood.

A person's discontent can be said to be represented by the distance between what they have and what they want. Once they have achieved what they want, the odds are good they will want still more, for that is the way of people, and that is a good healthy sign.

A person's world can be compared to a plot of ground. It exists and it has inherent within itself an amazing potential, which is prepared to react to mankind's every action.

Whatever your job happens to be, think of it for a moment as this plot of ground.

In the beginning, there is nothing there but earth. If a person sits and watches it, nothing will happen. If they toss a few seeds on it, the sun and the rain and the soil's natural fertility will combine to reward them with a few results for their limited efforts. Action = reaction. It all depends on just what they want from this plot of earth – and that is something they must decide first.

Let us say they want a beautiful lawn, bordered by flower gardens, with a big tree that they can one day sit under in the shade and admire their work.

So, they mark off the areas for the garden; cultivate, smooth and clean the soil of stones and rubbish; plant their lawn and their tree and their flowers. From this point on, anyone observing this plot of land can evaluate in a second the amount of service, the contribution, this person is giving to their project. How can you tell? You can tell by seeing what the land is giving back to the person.

Planting the plot is only the first step. We are given the plot and that is all we should be given. It is what we do with it that will determine its degree of greatness and success.

Today we are living in a new economy. The rules that we grew up with in business and industry no longer apply. If you study the individuals who have large prosperous organisations, you find that their focus is not on themselves or what they can get, but on their organisations, the people in them, and what they can do for them.

You cannot win in this system unless, and until, you help someone else win.

Each of us is given a plot to work – "a lifetime and the work we have chosen". Like the farmer, we will be grateful if we have the vision, imagination and intelligence to build well and successfully on the seemingly unimpressive land of our beginning. Or, we can let it fall into a haphazard condition with no real continuity or purpose behind it – with unpainted, ramshackle buildings, surrounded by weeds and debris. It is the same land, and it is what we do with it that makes the difference. The miracle is there – if only we are wise enough to see it and to realise that our fulfilment depends on our reaction to what we are given.

Once a person learns and obeys the natural laws, they will get rich – with mathematical certainty. There is but one great law: *Energy is.*

Unlike any other form of animal life that has been created, we were given the power of free will, and along with this power came certain responsibilities. The capacity to choose does not involve freedom from the consequence of our choices.

In the 21st century, in the artificial intelligence economy, we have two broad teaching options. Teach students the skills that are needed and risk them falling out of date or teach them to teach themselves the same skills as and when they need them. We need to help them to develop the ingenuity, adaptability and self-motivation to establish what is required and learn by themselves. This form of inside-out education can be achieved by understanding the power of the subconscious mind and the marvellous faculties of our human mind.

Success means ensuring the chance to master the tools we need to achieve our purpose, then help ourselves to understand the deeper principles of learning that underpin that process. Educating someone early to do one thing all of their lives is no longer the solution for the creation of success.

Today it is no longer matters what you know, but what you learn, and what you can do with it!

Rapid technological change, ever longer lives and the advancement of robots that many consider to be a threat to jobs, means there is a greater-than-ever need to pursue inside-out learning.

The learnt-it-all will always trump the know-it-all in the long run, even if they start with less innate capabilities, as opined by Microsoft CEO Satya Nadella. The learn-it-all sees talent as a result of consistent and relentless effort with persistence with the desired goal in mind all the time.

In the traditional education system of outside-in, a major part of testing via exams and bringing so-called discipline to students, stifles creativity. The outside-in education system was suitable after the Industrial Revolution. We once had use for massive work forces that would be willing to repeat daily tasks. We needed a population of those disciplined and able to work in factories to carry out arduous and undesirable tasks. But now such tasks are carried out by computers and robots.

The law has been written thousands of times by the greatest minds the world has produced, and as a result has appeared in many forms.

For our purposes it might be best be put this way: "Our rewards in life will always match our service."

If any person alive is discontented with their rewards, they should examine their service. Action results in Reaction. So simple, so basic, and yet so misunderstood.

Never in the history of the world have human beings been so interdependent. It is as impossible to live without serving others as it would be to live if others were not constantly serving us. This is good. The more closely knit this interdependence becomes, the greater will be human achievement. We need each other, and we literally cannot live without one another.

Martin Rutte, an American management consultant, says: "You have got to do it by yourself, and you can't do it alone."

But remember, whatever you seek in the form of rewards, you must first earn in the form of service to others. All attempts to sidestep this natural law will end in failure, frustration, and demoralisation.

CHAPTER 18

SEED FOR ACHIEVEMENT

In this chapter, I am going to introduce a principle that will substantially help you attain your personal and business goals and will result in your achieving a peace of mind you may never before have experienced.

Again, it seems that at least 95 percent of the people – maybe more – do not know about this, giving the person that does an enormous advantage.

For every cause, there will be an equal effect. If we make good use of our mind, abilities, and talents, this will become apparent in our outer lives. If we make the best use of our time, this too, will give us a great advantage, because only two or three people in a hundred really put their time to anywhere near its potential use.

This is being true to ourselves, because we are the only ones from whom we can steal time, talent, and ability. It is taking the time we have been given and putting it to our own good use. It is taking whatever abilities and talents we possess as separate and unique persons and putting them to their best use. In short: making the best use of what we have in the time we are given to use it. Sound simple? The truth is always simple and uncomplicated.

Truly successful people all have one thing in common: they all understand – consciously or unconsciously – the law of cause and effect, and they wisely work with it, instead of trying to work against it. In addition to everything else you have already learned, now consider that the real seed for achievement is truth and honesty.

Many of us have been conditioned, genetically and environmentally, to live one way – yet taught to live another. There are a great number of people who are so used to living with this conflict in their lives that they accept it as the norm. They may not even realise it is the cause of many of their problems, instead blaming other people, conditions and circumstances.

Most people believe they are honest and, with most situations in life, they probably are. If a cashier gives too much money back in change, the great majority of people will bring it to the cashier's attention. If a good friend shares something in confidence, it is only on rare occasions that their trust is betrayed.

However, when it comes to being honest with ourselves about why we do what we do, and why we do not do some of the things we would like to do, it is a different matter. Earl Nightingale talks about this eloquently in his book, *Lead the Field*. Most people become extremely effective at lying to themselves.

If you surveyed the most effective people you know, you would find they are masters of being honest with themselves and are mentally strong. As a result, they continually develop their talents and abilities. Being truthful with ourselves means taking responsibility for making the best use of what we have. The choice is ours, and it is here that personal honesty and integrity come into the picture.

There are numerous definitions of integrity, such as: "A person has integrity when their thoughts, their feelings and their actions are all in harmony."

Consider the conditioning that has taken place in a person's subconscious mind and how, because of this conditioning, a person's thoughts, feelings and actions are frequently not in sync.

This is the foundation on which every great career is built – integrity, trust and honesty are the keys to success. Honesty is good business. In fact, the French revolutionary Mirabeau once wrote: "If honesty did not exist, we ought to invent it as the best means of getting rich. It is the only way on earth to real and lasting success of any kind."

Integrity has higher value than loyalty. In fact, integrity is the highest form of loyalty. We have integrity if our thoughts, feelings, and actions are all in harmony.

Integrity also means being integrated on principles, which Steven Covey relates to the law of nature, and to people organisations, or even family members.

When we prioritise being loyal to a person or a group over doing what we feel to be right, we lose integrity. We may temporarily gain popularity or build false loyalty, but this loss of your principle and violation of the law of nature, will eventually undermine even those relationships.

Over time integrity produces loyalty. If you attempt to reverse them and go for loyalty first at times, you may find yourself compromising your integrity and may violate the laws of nature. It's better to be trusted than to be liked. Ultimately trust and respect will generally facilitate the *creation of success.*

All we have to do under every circumstance is ask whether we are being true to ourselves. Only then can we go ahead with the happy realisation that we have taken care of the cause – and the effect will take care of itself.

Although most people will give lip-service to honesty, they are really not at all sure about it. With the great majority, it is a matter of expediency. If it is more expedient to realise a quick profit in some way by not disclosing the whole truth or by shading it a bit – well, they will hide it a bit. Why? Because they live on a short term, instant gratification basis. They do not see living as a long-term arrangement. They forget – or do not know – about what Earl Nightingale liked to call "the unfailing boomerang".

Every time a person does something dishonest, whether it is small or large, whether it is stealing a pair of pliers from the plant or embezzling a few thousand pounds, or whether it is selling themselves short by not making full use of their time, talents, and abilities, they are throwing the boomerang. How far it will travel, no one knows.

How great or how small a circle it will traverse, only time will tell. But it will eventually, inevitably, come around behind that person to deliver its never failing and painful blow.

Yes – honesty is good business. It is the only way on earth to real and lasting success of any kind. Either we are convinced of this – with every fibre of our being – totally and completely, or we are not. If we do not know this by the time we are adults, then we deserve every knock we get. In fact, if we did not deserve them, we would not get them.

There is little doubt that workers in the free world have much greater earning power than those in a closed society. Yet it is a mistake to think that we cannot receive more than we earn. What you put in, you get back, whether that is in thoughts, feelings or actions. Sometimes people fail to realise that things happen because we have ordered them. We choose our thoughts, words and actions or paradigms. These paradigms cause people to let go of what they know is true.

If you think back to your formative years, consider how the people you were surrounded by used their time. Their habits would naturally have become your habits but of course, you can change your own paradigm. Our thoughts and ideas have been formed by the energy that flows through us. The reason you are drawn to one thought or idea, instead of another, is because of your paradigm which are programmed into each and every one of us. But it is critical to remember that free will rules. Sometimes compromise is required and compromise can cause ripples.

Cause and effect shows us that when we are dishonest we are punished; if we act justly we will reap rewards. The greatest joy is that of achievement. You have more talent and ability than you imagine, you just need to make use of it before time passes you by.

Living successfully is a matter of forming the right habits, one of the most important of which is honesty in everything we do. Despite this, each year, in every country in the world, employees take home billions of pounds worth of unauthorised company merchandise or property.

It is estimated that the same amount is taken, but undetected and not reported for many reasons. This is a grand total in the billions and billions of pounds stolen from employers. It is seldom even thought of in this way by the average employee who helps themselves.

But the monetary loss from company thefts is nothing compared to the loss from another kind of theft: the theft of productivity or wasting time. In both cases it at first appears that only the employer suffers, but this is not really true. The employee is hurt most. They are stealing productive time from their company, and while this hurts, the company will not likely fail just because of that person. More important is the fact that the employee is stealing opportunity from themselves, thereby holding themselves back and limiting themselves.

That person grows smaller and fails, unless and until they wake up. *Honesty really is all.*

CHAPTER 19

LEVEL OF AWARENESS

According to the work of Bob Proctor, there are seven levels of awareness: **Animal, Mass, Aspiration, Individual, Discipline, Experience** and Mastery.

At the first level – the *Animal* level – it is fight or flight, putting an individual in a 'reactionary' mode.

The next level – *Mass* consciousness – is where an individual, without thinking, steps into the crowd and obediently follows wherever the crowd leads. Then comes *Aspiration*, when an individual starts to read and listen to quality information and becomes aware that they may be capable of more than they had at first thought.

Individual awareness comes when, after aspiring to something better, a person begins to acknowledge the amazing things that they are capable of.

Then comes *Discipline*, which provides the force to propel the individual to break away from the mass level of awareness and do more. As the individual applies discipline and works to move to new levels, the *Experience* gained reinforces their awareness of their own abilities. Let us consider discipline: when we are at school, what the teachers ask us to do is not discipline, but is rather conforming and, at times, punishment. Here, the discipline is to give yourself a command and then follow it.

And finally comes the *Mastery* level, when there is a higher level of thought, and the person stops and thinks, and then thinks and responds. At the animalistic level we react - at the mastery level, we respond.

Seven Levels Of Awareness

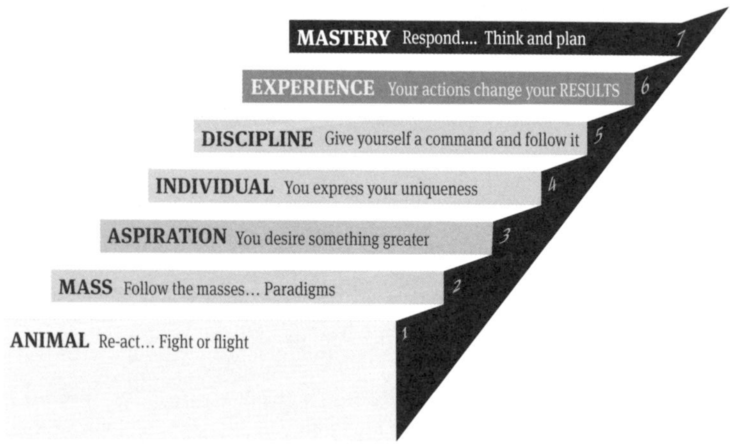

Let us stop right here and examine what is happening from a psychological perspective. To do this we need to revisit the model of our mind, the stick person.

The conscious mind reasons both inductively and deductively, while the sub-conscious mind is totally deductive. Inductive reasoning is where we go from the specific to the general. In other words, we think a thought, we add it to another thought, then another thought, and as we keep adding thoughts we build the idea. This is, in truth, what is referred to as thinking.

The inductive reasoning factor in the personality is what we think with. When it is not working, the mind is in a totally deductive state and the personality is totally subjective to whatever thought or ideas happen to be present.

Consider for a moment what kind of actions a person would be involved in where there was nothing but ideas of lack, limitation, jealousy, resentment and blame circulating. It would be nothing short of a miracle for a person in that position to break out of that environment, become aware of the cause of their behaviour and results to alter their paradigm or their conditioning and improve the quality of their life. Although the odds may be great against such an individual, there are numerous people who do it and anyone can.

The famous American pastor, Harry Emerson Fosdick, once wrote: "No horse gets anywhere until he is harnessed. No steam or gas ever drives anything until it is confined. No Niagara is ever turned into light and power until it is channelled. And no life ever grows great until it is focused, dedicated, disciplined."

It is actually easier to succeed – all we have to do is know some of the rules and follow them.

The British author Philip Gilbert Hamerton wrote: "A strong life is like a ship of war, which has its own place in the fleet, and can share in its strength and discipline but can also go forth alone to the solitude of the infinite sea. We ought to belong to society and have our place in it, but be capable of an individual existence, outside of it."

And it is never too late. For with a purpose – a goal – a person will frequently do more and travel farther in a year than they might in a lifetime without one.

First, we must begin to think. We must look at ourselves objectively for what we really are; distinct individuals with unlimited opportunities for development.

The next stage is to ask ourselves some critical questions, as illustrated by Earl Nightingale, such as: "Do I want to be like the people I am following? Are these the people I want my children to be like? Do they know where they are going? Are they successful? Are they as successful as I want to be? If I continue to go along as I have in the past, where will I be in five years from now? Am I operating at or near peak efficiency? Am I really a professional, or have I been doing just enough to get by?"

I expect my company, my community and my country to improve with the passing of each year. But what am I doing, personally, to keep pace with this improvement, or to exceed it? Have I thought much – and told my children – about how lucky we are to live in a free society in which we can go where we please without having to ask for permission, work where we please in the job of our choice, vote and worship as we please and say what we please?

Am I aware of the responsibilities that go with freedom, to produce as much as I can so my freedom may be maintained, to become so effective as a person that even if times should become bad for a while, I could go right on providing for my family through the crisis?

All kinds of studies have been done into motivation, and what it is that motivates people to do the things they do, live the way they live and achieve the goals they achieve. I believe the overriding force that motivates us, as persons, is something I call choice of environment, with environment being the immediate world we are surrounded by.

Some people make this choice consciously, but I am certain the great majority of people make the choice unconsciously as a result of environmental conditioning.

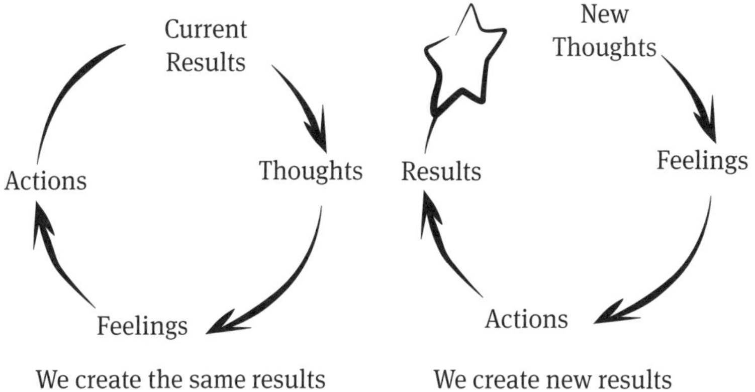

When you look at your results and let the results register in your mind, the results cause you to think. The thinking produces the feeling, the feeling causes the action and the action produces the result — the same result. This is precisely why the majority of our population keep getting the same results, year after year. It's called "struggle".

Immediately stop permitting the outside world to control your mind. Objectively observe what is going on in your outside world. Do not be a part of it. Look at your results as a stranger might. Say: "Hmm, I don't think that's what I want." Then begin to think about what you do want.

Think thoughts that will create the idea of what you want. The thoughts cause the feelings, the feelings cause the actions and the action produces a new result. At that point, you consciously observe the new result; you mentally adapt to the new results and immediately begin to think the thoughts that create the idea of how to improve upon it.

Remember, it starts with the thought. The thought causes the feeling, the feeling causes the action, the action causes the result. Take a look at the result, adapt, and start a new train of thought. You stay in charge of you. Do not let the outside world control you. You control the outside world.

Every person in reality is in business for themselves in that they are building their own life.

While the operation of a business is multitudinous and complex, they can be reduced to four basic functions:

1. Finance
2. Production
3. Sales
4. Research

Without proper financing, there would be no production. Without production, the company would have nothing to sell. Without sales, it would have to completely stop production. Without research it could not hop to keep abreast or ahead of our rapidly changing times.

Now, if any of these four vital functions are not working in harmony, you will have a deformed, crippled company, and if you leave it long enough, you'll commit corporate suicide.

Your corporation and your life have two factors to consider; the present and the future. How successful we are in meeting these challenges will determine our present profits and our future growth.

Why are all companies concerned with growth, even when they seem to be doing well today? It is because of a law that operates with companies, just as it does with human beings. Nothing in the world stands still. Nothing in the entire universe stands still. A law of physics dictates:

'A body in motion tends to remain in motion, until acted upon by an outside force.'

A company that is growing has a tendency to continue to grow. Conversely, a company that is going backwards, or shrinking, tends to continue to go backwards, or shrink, until acted upon by an outside force.

All responsible leaders know that unless a company is growing, it is developing the first signs of death. Well – you're the head of your personal corporation and you should realise that the same law applies to you as well.

Never before, through all of the centuries of humanity, has a person faced as bright a future as ours. Our population isn't just exploding, it is getting a lot smarter.

Educational advances in the last century have been remarkable, during the next few decades to 2050 they will be amazing.

The customer is getting smarter every day. And if we are going to continue to meet their demands, and sell to them our products or services, we need to increase our awareness and get smarter every day too. Because, if we don't they are not going to buy from us.

The market of the next few decades will be characterised by diversity – not uniformity. It will be dominated by taste, not necessity. There will be a great increase in the quality, as well as the quantity of consumer choices.

There are many signs of the rising urge in which the USA, which will filter down to the UK and rest of the world for life long learning and enabling the work force to deal with the technological changes including artificial intelligence. Many millions of adults are currently interested in life-long learning and searching for knowledge to enhance their awareness and this number is growing in millions by the year.

People who operate with a fixed mind-set, as per research, are more likely to stick to activities that they have already studied and mastered, rather than the embarrassment of failing on some new innovation. People focused on growth and indeed creation of success, make it their mission to learn new knowledge, understanding that they will not succeed at all of them at first.

Carol Dweck, in her bestseller, Mindset – The New Psychology of Success, divides the world into learners and non-learners. The fixed mindset will limit you and the growth mindset can move you forward. This concept helped Microsoft CEO Satya Nadella to improve the share price substantially and grow Microsoft to a leading global company.

CHAPTER 20

ONE THING YOU CANNOT HIDE

One thing that is incredibly important as we embark on our educational, professional and personal journeys is the power of language, and knowing our own language. More people speak English now than any other language, with the possible exception of Chinese, and perhaps very soon Hindi.

Our language in the United Kingdom, United States, Canada, Australia and many other countries, is English and we need to continuously improve our command of the English language every day – well beyond the end of our studies.

Even if your country does not have English as its first language, learning English is just as critical for success.

English literature, from Chaucer to Eliot, from Shakespeare to Hemingway, is the richest and most extensive on earth. When you are studying English, you are studying one of the world's greatest and most interesting subjects.

If you think you do not have time to study, listen to what the noted librarian Louis Shores had to say: "Each of us must find their own 15-minute period each day for reading." It's better if it is regular. The only requirement is the will to read. With it you can find 15 minutes, no matter how busy the day. That means you will read half a book a week, two books a month, 20 a year… and 1,000 in a reading lifetime. It's an easy way to become well read and well educated, giving up just 15 minutes a day.

What we read is also important. Everyone has something in which they have a general interest. This is true of the salesman, doctor, architect, executive, lawyer, teacher, accountant, politician, student or housewife. Reading in this area is for gain, and we should read for pleasure as well.

Once we have an ongoing, regular programme to improve our knowledge of our language, we should begin a systematic study of the field that interests us most and that will help us reach our goal just that much sooner.

To try to live without constantly expanding our knowledge is to close our eyes, not just to the whole purpose of life, but to the facts of life as well. Never before has the world moved so rapidly as it is moving today. We must make up our mind to move with it – to stay up with it – to grow and prosper with it. Not just because it is the best way to our goals, but because it is the way to really enjoy living, as the skilful sailor enjoys the sea.

So often a person will live in the shallows, which we call paradigms, from force of habit or because those around them are wasting their time there. They don't realise that only a thin screen of reeds separates them from the fine, deep ocean beyond. That person can sail to any port of their choosing if they take the time, and expend the effort, to build a good boat.

This is an important point. The person who knows where they are going, and who has made up their mind to get there, is going to make it, regardless of their education, experience and family origins. If an education is necessary to the accomplishment of their goal, they will get it. They will achieve their business goals, regardless of the challenges thrown in their way. Nothing in the world can take the place of persistence and determination.

It is important to succeed in every department of our lives – and becoming well educated and widely read is one of the most vital. What good is a large material success if a person has remained too ignorant to enjoy it, or to administer it?

Knowledge is power, and the greater our knowledge, the more power we can exercise over our lives - and our futures. Think of human society as a pyramid, composed of layers. Pick the place on the pyramid you are going to shoot for and start climbing.

We acquire the skills we need to live successfully through knowledge. Knowledge, properly applied, is power, and knowledge is available to all of us, but we need to study regularly; not just for examinations, but to improve our understanding of the world around us and to eliminate ignorance. We ignore great opportunities in life too often as a result of ignorance.

The degree of a person's ignorance will determine their place in the world. Everyone is born ignorant and must, for a time, live in ignorance. But anyone who remains ignorant has only themselves to blame. An illiterate person in our society is on the bottom rung of the ladder. At the very peak of the pyramid are the world's most brilliant people. We may not all have the desire to reach the uppermost pinnacle, although we certainly can if we want to, but we do control where we live between the top and the bottom.

Think about an egg. If pressure is applied to an egg from the outside, it will break and end its life. If pressure is applied from the inside, however, the egg will hatch and create life. Here, the inside-out education is creation, while the outside-in education can be disrupting. This is evidenced by the world as it exists today. We need to embrace inside-out education as illustrated by Clayton M. Christensen, the man who came up with the hugely influential theory of 'disruptive innovation'.

We can, most assuredly, get into the top one percent.

It is not about being above others, but rather about having the ambition and good sense to live as best we can. It is wholly our choice – we give ourselves a command and we follow it, that is the discipline and disruptive power of inside-out education.

The higher you climb on the pyramid, the further you can see, the fresher the air, the better the view and the less crowded it becomes.

Another rewarding thing about climbing is that as we climb, we help most of those associated with us to climb too. This is why teams are so important – the most successful organisations are run by extremely effective teams, with the utmost integrity in leadership.

One of the most important ladders leading us to the top is knowledge, because the more we know, the higher we can move.

But, no one can know everything. In fact, the world's store of knowledge is growing too fast for anyone to ever keep up with it. So, a person should begin with the study of their language, and then their areas of interest and career or profession. Just those two steps can move us high up the pyramid.

Not enough people realise that it is our ability to use our language that will determine our place on the social pyramid and will control, to a significant extent, our journey in life.

A person can dress in the latest fashion and present an attractive appearance, but the minute they open their mouth and speak they proclaim to the world their level on the pyramid. George Bernard Shaw's play, *Pygmalion*, later adapted into the musical comedy *My Fair Lady*, is a perfect example. Our use of the language is the one thing we cannot hide.

To try to live without constantly expanding our knowledge is to close our eyes, not just to the whole purpose of life, but to the facts of life as well. Never has the world moved so rapidly as it is moving today. We must make up our mind to move with it, and to grow and prosper alongside it, not just because it is the best way to our goals, but because it is the way to really enjoy our lives.

Realise that finishing secondary school and graduating from university with your undergraduate and postgraduate qualifications, or even doing your PhD or doctorate, is just the beginning of a journey of learning. With wisdom comes kindness, patience, love, understanding, and success and self-fulfilment. It is never too late to begin.

CHAPTER 21

THE END OF EDUCATION IS CHARACTER

James Allen, a great Harvard professor, explains character as follows: "As a man thinketh in his heart so is he." In other words, we are what we think, with our character being the composite of all thoughts.

Every human act springs from the hidden seeds of thoughts, as the plant springs from the seed. Acts can be spontaneous and unpremeditated or deliberately executed.

Thoughts trigger actions, and success and suffering are the results. Thoughts make us who we are and shape our character. If our mind entertains unpleasant thoughts, we are destined for unhappiness, but if, on the other hand, we have pleasant thoughts, joy and success should surely follow.

Man is a growth - not a creation; cause and effect are absolute. A noble and peaceful character is not a thing of chance but the natural result of continual and consistent effort in positive thinking. The opposite is also true.

We are made or unmade by ourselves. Through our thoughts, we forge the weapons by which we are able to destroy ourselves. By making the correct choices we can increase our awareness and create success, or by making bad choices we can disintegrate our achievements. Between these two pillars of life are all the grades of character, and we are their maker and master.

Albert Einstein explains this concept of character, saying: "The intuitive or emotional mind is a sacred gift and the rational or educated mind is a faithful servant. We have created a society that honours the servant and has forgotten the gift."

As beings of power, intelligence and owners of our own thoughts, we hold the key to every situation and contain within ourselves that transforming and regenerative power by which we make ourselves what we want to be and with which to build a strong character. We are masters of our own destiny, and even when we are at our weakest we have the power to search diligently, to become wiser, and to direct our energies with intelligence.

Only by much searching and mining are gold and diamonds obtained, and we can find every truth connected with our being if we dig deep into our minds and become the makers of our own characters, the moulder of our lives and the builders of our destiny.

In this direction, we can build a solid character. The end of education is character, but education never ends. Education needs to do more than just develop curiosity and enquiring minds, it must cultivate a commitment to self-improvement and promote constant learning, and the idea of life-long learning.

Character is what allows you to reach the top and stay there. Psychologist Carol Dweck, in her bestseller, *Mindset*, illustrates the point when she quotes: "I believe ability can get you to the top, but it takes the character to keep you there. It is so easy if you understand the basic law of cause and effect. Character being the *effect* and *thinking* is the cause. Start to think respecting the natural laws. You can just turn it on automatically."

Successful people, who can maintain for a long period of time at this level possess. More than ability they have character. Building character can be a process, and in this book I have explained this within the chapters. In order to achieve success, we need to create results, following the same law of nature; results are the *effect* and *habit* is the cause. Our deep routed habits are our paradigms which need to change if we need to change the results and get to where we want to be.

Sound character will keep us at that position during our lifetime. We can all think about various successful people who were once very successful, and either not in the history books or completing the final stages of their lives in misery or ill-health, and some even in confined prisons as a result of the law or their own action.

Today, a formal education system provided by institutions sees teachers and lecturers organising the learning experience for students, who are sub-divided into classes or lecture groups. Most of the world is still working to a modified version of the educational system, which is based on the Third Education Revolution, dating back to the 17th century, as identified by historian Sir Anthony Seldon.

Yet the world has changed so drastically since then, particularly in the 21st century, and now the education system is about to enter the Fourth Education Revolution. The power of technology, the rise of new ways of learning and the growth of the internet impart powerful new opportunities for us to become our own teachers.

Much of the debate in the United Kingdom today over the role of character formation in schools and universities revolves around the purpose of education. But it is increasingly clear that shaping character is a necessary and vital aspect of education. As Harvard Professor Howard Gardner once said: "Don't ask how intelligent a child is, ask how a child is intelligent."

The definition of intelligence is changing, and in the Fourth Educational Revolution, all educators will have to work out whether artificial intelligence is going to liberate or infantilise humanity. Sir Anthony Seldon, who is also the Vice-Chancellor of the University of Buckingham, recently published a fascinating book on this very topic and Dr Rami Ranger, in his book *From Nothing to Everything*, emphasised the need for character-building and pointed out that the secret to success is integrity, honesty and good character.

A fully educated person has a thirst for knowledge and a curiosity that stays with them.

Napoleon Hill, the American author who has influenced millions of people in education in respect of human potential and human evolution, said: "An educated person is not necessarily one who has an abundance of general or specialist knowledge. An educated person is one who has developed the faculties of their mind so that they may acquire anything that they want without violating the rights of others."

My late father, Senior Selvanayagam, inspired me with a very simple message, told to him by his father, my grandfather.

He said: "I do not want to say my son is an educated doctor, lawyer or accountant, or a successful entrepreneur or business leader, I want to say my son has great character." My late father was a wonderful man.

We have a responsibility to consider new ways of educating the human race across the world because, as the former British Prime Minister, Winston Churchill, once said: "Responsibility is the price of greatness." Responsibility means our ability to respond, not to react.

Regent Group was created with the ethos *The end of education is character*, and, after nearly two decades of growth, we have a proven methodology that my lovely wife and business partner Tharshiny and I, hope will create a world that is a better place than it was when we were born in the 1970s. Education needs to be about building character and giving the next generation the confidence and freedom to go where their hearts lead them, to do the best they can do, and be the best that they can be.

Do take the time to read and re-read the chapters as many times as you can. Repetition is critical to shifting paradigms, when supported by deep emotions and underpinned by laws of nature.

I trust you are already implementing these principles to your daily life and seeing the amazing life-changing results they bring. Learn to do practical things and develop your marvellous mind. Thomas Edison knew that the mind could produce anything that the mind could conceive and believe, and that knowledge was the thing that lifted the great Edison above the common human.

Henry Ford once said: "I'll belt the earth with dependable motor cars." He did, with his marvellous mind; his decision to trust his own judgement revolutionised the global automotive industry.

For those seeking similar success, let it be remembered that practically the sole difference between Henry Ford and the majority of the more than 100,000 staff that worked for him was this – he had a mind and controlled it, and others had minds that they did not try to control.

Inside-out education will enhance your character by controlling your mind, because character building is linked to mind control. Mind control is the result of self-discipline and changing paradigms. You either control your mind, or it controls you – there is no compromise.

The most practical of all methods for controlling the mind is the habit of keeping it busy with a definite purpose, a worthy goal, backed by a definite and organised plan. Study the record of any human that achieves noteworthy success and you will see they have unwavering control of their mind. Moreover, they exercise that control and direct it towards the attainment of a definite purpose.

Control the mind and you can achieve anything, as long as it is worthy of you. This is the proven methodology for the creation of success and self-fulfilment.

Thinking into Character: Virtual Learning Platform

If you enjoyed reading this book, and would like to re-visit the content though a series of videos and linked workbooks, or feel this may be of interest to a friend, please visit our website at www.tic.uk.com